The Kenai Catastrophe

by

Michael T. Barbour

Ricky and Diana,
Thanks for your support.
Enjoy! MTBarbour
23Dec02

i

The Kenai Catastrophe

U.S.A. & International
Copyright © 2002 Michael T. Barbour
All rights reserved
ISBN 0-9705593-2-1

Published and Distributed by:
Rebel Publishing
PO Box 90037
Sioux Falls, SD 57109
U.S.A.

First Printing September 2002

The Kenai Catastrophe

Acknowledgements

Thanks to Malcolm Macpherson for his advice and guidance throughout the lengthy process of writing, preparing the manuscript for review, and obtaining an agent. My deepest appreciation to friends who offered invaluable insights and feedbacks to the storyline — especially Elaine, Susan, Florence, Karen, Anna, Dave. And, special appreciation to my wife's support and reading the full manuscript. I am indebted to Kay Garrett of Professional Editing Services, who patiently led me through all the pitfalls of sentence structure, narrator viewpoint, meandering prose, etc. My sincere gratitude to Michael Cox of Rebel Publishing and his assistant, Val Kallas, for their belief in me and their dedication to improving my manuscript to the highest standards. My son, Brent, designed the cover for the book, and demonstrated his artistic side. My other son, Kurt, designed and continues to maintain my website at www.michaeltbarbour.com.

The Kenai Catastrophe
Table of Contents

Chapter 1

The Everglades

The two men in the airboat were intent on their route and on not falling out, as it skimmed across the Everglades. Zigzagging in and out of the marsh grass to avoid sandbars, sometimes erratically, the driver was always in control. With his backward ball cap and his tinted goggles, he looked perhaps less concerned than he really was.

The passenger, Chad Gunnings, crouched in the bow and grasped a rope tied to the flattened cleat in the bow. He had been in the Everglades for nearly three months. His composure belied his discomfort as he and the driver skimmed at breakneck speed through the tall marsh grass. Chad occasionally gave furtive glances behind him to gauge the distance between his boat and the one pursuing him and his partner. He held tight to the rope with one hand while moving from side to side searching ahead to help the driver choose the best course of escape.

Both he and Red, the driver, had earphones and a gooseneck mic attached to a wireless 65 transmitter so they could correspond over the high-pitched scream of the jet fan powering the airboat. Chad would shout his sightings of isolated hummocks of mud that could do real damage to the airboat. Red was usually already aware of the hummocks from his high perch on his pedestal seat.

Although Chad was concerned about their predicament, he marveled at the ability of his friend to maneuver the powerful airboat in and out of narrow channels, over shallow areas and through the thick marsh grass. Their escape from the boat holding three men with guns was dependent on his partner's executing difficult and somewhat reckless maneuvers around and over impossible obstacles. Red worked to maintain distance. Occasionally, the trailing boat would gain; however, Red always managed to execute a quick turn or accelerate to pull ahead. Neither of the men had guns. Their purpose for being in the Everglades was to conduct an environmental study.

They were investigating the ecological effects of the severe drought conditions due to a combination of an extraordinarily dry year and the absence of drainage from the upper section of the Everglades resulting from the construction of diversion canals. They never thought they would encounter drug runners this far north in the 'Glades.

Chad and Red had been moving slowly down a side channel taking plankton samples with a small cone-shaped net that Chad was dragging just below the surface. As they came around a clump of tall marsh grass, they startled two airboats full of men—three in one and two in the other.

Chad looked up. "Hi, there," he said. But before he could say more, all but one man pulled guns out of their jackets and waistbands.

Red was familiar with the 'Glades and knew instantly that this was a drug transaction. He turned the boat swiftly, almost knocking Chad out of the boat as he was withdrawing the net from the water. Red accelerated quickly and swerved across the marsh grass barrier into a larger and deeper channel, heading back the way they had come. Bullets were whizzing overhead and into the shallow water next to their boat as the three men in one of the boats took up pursuit. The second boat with the senior member of the drug transaction went in the opposite direction. The swiftness of the reaction of the drug pushers indicated that this was either a very sensitive transaction or that Chad and Red were thought to be officers from the Drug Enforcement Agency.

Chad shouted above the noise of the airboat engine. "Are these men the same who we fought a couple weeks back?"

"I didn't get a good look," Red responded. "It could just be a coincidence. These drug activities are commonplace here in the 'Glades. Without helicopters and powerful chase boats, the authorities are hard-pressed to curtail the illegal activities in the 'Glades."

As Chad and Red made their escape, Chad thought back on the previous run-in with drug runners earlier in the season. It happened when Red was loading the airboat with supplies for their day's survey. Two men confronted him with drawn guns and demanded that Red take them into the Everglades. Chad remembered their surprise when he came up behind the men. The men turned to face Chad, the guns leveled ominously on him. Without hesitation, Chad leaped towards the men. This move surprised the men. Before they could shoot, he threw double sidekicks at the men, his left foot connecting with one man's sternum, and his right foot hitting the second man in the face. His martial arts training had been helpful more than once in the past. His forceful kicks sent both men sprawling. Red helped him to dispatch the men, preventing any shots from being fired.

Chad didn't think the men now chasing them were connected to the men he and Red had fought a couple of weeks before. Regardless, now both he and Red were running for their lives. Red maneuvered the airboat from left to right, seemingly careening out of control. He left the main channel in favor of the more secluded side channels and narrow pathways that were prevalent throughout the 'Glades. These maneuvers were dangerous because of the risk of hitting submerged logs, gators, or emergent hummocks of dirt and mud. However, the pursuing men were unable to fire their pistols. Red and Chad were traveling at a high rate of speed, and their path of escape was solely up to Red's instincts and knowledge of the 'Glades. Suddenly, Red swerved to the right to avoid four alligators on a small hummock of mud and marsh grass. The men in the pursuing airboat were surprised by the quick maneuvers and, spotting the gators, swerved to the left. The boat missed the gators by a narrow margin. The men turned the boat in the direction that Red and Chad had taken and began closing the gap. Red continued in this new direction, which was away from the dock and civilization where they hoped to find help. Chad did not question Red's move, because he trusted his friend's instincts and suspected he might have a plan to secure their escape. They were quickly coming to a berm, which separated the canal that served as a narrow conveyance system used to drain land for agriculture from the Everglades. Red shouted to Chad to hang on and accelerated to maximum speed. Rather than swerving to parallel it, Red aimed directly at the berm where the airboat swept up and over as if launched and became airborne. They cleared the canal and landed in the wetlands beyond, almost dislodging Red from his perch and making Chad look like he was riding a wild bronco.

Without any thought of strategy, the men in the second airboat followed the first over the berm. However, the men in the boat were not as ready to endure the flight as Chad and Red. As their boat was launched over the berm, one man was thrown high into the air, his 9mm pistol discharging harmlessly as he flailed. He was dumped unceremoniously into the canal, disturbing two alligators who were nestled in the margins of the canal. The second man fell into the boat, but hung on to his gun. The driver was the only one in the second boat who was able to maintain control over his balance and the boat.

Chad noted that Red's surprise move and his neat execution of the jump gained them precious meters in the escape attempt.

Red continued to zigzag through the wetlands and canals, hoping to lose their pursuer.

Chad was desperately trying to think of a solution to their predicament. The facts were not encouraging: they had no gun; they were not close to a location where the police could be reached; they didn't have a cellular phone; and they were not near any public place that would discourage the use of guns. Their only hope was to out-maneuver or out-distance the other boat. Chad knew that the other men had figured out that he and Red were not from the DEA. These men were ruthless — that was certain. Chad wondered why these men didn't give a second thought to their lost companion. Back in the conveyance canal, the man may or may not be conscious and able to escape the alligators that were very abundant in the Everglades.

With the distance gained temporarily, Red slowed so he could ascertain the whereabouts of the other boat and hopefully hide from the pursuers. He didn't hear the high-pitched whine of the other boat's airplane engine, and thought that they had perhaps succeeded in escaping the pursuers. Red maintained the slow pace and engine at idle as he kept to the margins of the tall, dense wetland vegetation.

Chad did a quick inventory of their equipment to determine if a weapon could be fabricated from the various scientific equipment and tools. Chad's martial arts training was now taking over from his scientific background, and he was thinking in terms of defense. He was an accomplished black belt in the art of Tae Kwon Do, having studied continuously through his high school and college days. He remembered his master's teachings of how a weapon could be anything and that it was essentially an extension of one's body. The strategy of weaponry was to make it one with the body, and that 'thrusts and parries' were best executed from the core of the body where the chi (or energy) is centered. The potential weapons were meager—a long-handled net used to collect organisms off the substrate and from the submerged vegetation, an instrument used to collect water quality data and consisting of a relatively heavy plastic cylinder housing various sensors and connected to a rubberized cable, the small net used for plankton, and miscellaneous jars and paraphernalia used to conduct scientific surveys.

Just as Chad was completing his survey of the equipment, the second boat suddenly rounded the bend in the wetland in front of them and headed straight for them. Red accelerated—the boat leaping forward directly in the path of the second boat. This maneuver startled the drug runners, throwing off the concentration of the man in the bow who was pointing the pistol at Chad and Red. In a split second the boats were side-by-side, and Chad flipped a box of plastic jars in the face of the man in the bow. The man threw up his hands. This allowed Red to quickly pass the other boat and head straight out to the main channel beyond. The second boat turned, and the race was on again.

Red directed the airboat toward a cypress swamp on the margin of the wetland area of the Everglades.

Chad hoped that the darkness of the swamp and its inherent hazards would discourage the other men. Perhaps if Red could lead the men into the poor visibility of the dense cypress swamp, the barely submerged cypress knees would damage the hull of the unsuspecting boat and this would provide an escape opportunity.

The man in the bow of the second boat holstered his pistol and picked up a rifle. Through his headset radio, Chad yelled, "Watch it Red. He has a rifle." Red heeded the warning and re-initiated his maneuvering to make it harder for the man to aim. The man took several shots in a desperate attempt to stop them from entering the swamp. One bullet struck the metal gunnel at the stern of the boat, and a second bounced off the metal cage of the large propeller.

They reached the cypress swamp and darted in among the

trees, whose trunks were fully submerged in the dark water. The real danger was the unknown extent of the woody knees that were submerged and extended from the cypress trees. Red seemed to know where he was going, darting in and out of the tree stands and somehow avoiding the cypress knees, most of which were submerged below the water line. The darkness and closeness of the trees prevented any further shooting. The pursuit continued down the dark corridors of the swamp. The passages were becoming more narrow, and Red had to greatly reduce the boat's speed. Suddenly, there was no way to go. A large cypress had fallen in the last storm, blocking the narrow passageway. Red and Chad turned hoping to exit the way they came before the other boat could effectively block their escape.

Before Red and Chad could reach one of the side channels, the second boat was upon them. The man in the bow was grinning at their predicament and pointing his gun at them. "Where do you think you're going?" He said.

"We just realized that we were out of beer and were returning to the store," Chad replied.

"I don't think so," the man said. "I think you will be here for a while — a long while, in fact." He laughed.

The boats were now within a meter of each other with the engines at idle. The man with the rifle looked as if he were enjoying himself. Chad was holding the long-handled net. He could tell by the look in the man's eyes that he recognized the collecting net for what it was. The man laughed again. "So, you out catchin' bugs?"

"That's right, sir," Chad said.

The man didn't seem to notice Chad's formality, and asked, "Let's see what you got there in them jars."

Chad looked down and out of the corner of his eye saw a water moccasin gliding at the surface of the water between the boats. As Chad bent over to seemingly reach for a jar, he swept the net smoothly and quickly in an arc from its upright position through the water, capturing the snake. Continuing the arc with the net so that the centrifugal force would hold the snake in the net, Chad turned his body around in a semicircle and used his weight as a fulcrum and flipped the net artfully so that the snake continued in its flight directly in the lap of the driver. Chad continued the follow-through of the net so that the pole was then brought into a position level with the gut of the man with the rifle. For a split second, the man with the rifle was frozen, watching in shock at the snake flying toward his partner. In that momentary lapse of attention, Chad thrust the pole into the man's midsection, knocking him from the boat and into some jutting cypress knees, which cracked a couple of ribs and immobilized him.

The driver convulsed with the snake in his lap and inadvertently accelerated the boat erratically toward a cypress stand. The boat rammed into one tree and bounced, becoming slightly airborne, and landing on a clump of cypress knees. The hull buckled, preventing any further movement. With this distraction, the snake managed to escape somewhere in the swamp, but not before leaving some of its venom in the thigh of the driver. The driver fell to the bottom of the boat moaning and writhing in pain.

Red drove the boat closer, so that Chad could check on the driver and ensure that no further retaliation was possible from these drug runners. Chad jumped to the other boat and removed all of the guns and ammunition. He and Red carefully extracted the wounded man from the cypress knees, bandaged him as best they could and put him in the airboat with the snake-bitten driver. Red hitched a rope to the other airboat and they began towing the boat with the injured drug runners out of the cypress swamp. Chad found a cellular phone among the heap of equipment and metal briefcases full of white powder. He used the phone to call the police and report the incident, providing the location for the pick-up of the men.

When Chad flipped the phone closed, he looked at Red. "Well, Red -- how about that beer?"

Red grinned as he turned the boat to head out of the swamp. He thought, "Yes, it is going to be rather dull around here when that boy leaves for home."

Chapter 2

Phoenix Environmental
Research Institute

The jetliner was cruising at 10,000 meters above the cloud cover. Chad looked out from his window seat, musing about the solid appearance of the thick clouds and how they looked like a blanket of snow. It was sunny where he was, high over the Appalachian Mountains, but raining down below onto the lush vegetation of the mountains.

It would be good to get home. It was May, and he was returning after a three-month sampling trip to the Everglades. The environmental study was near completion, and he only had to report back to the institute and to write up his findings on the effects of the drought conditions on the ecology of the Everglades. His assistant, Joslyn Brown, had returned almost three weeks earlier to begin writing the report. She was a very capable scientist and had joined him at the institute shortly after graduating from Morgan State University in Baltimore. That was two years ago. Now, she had become Chad's right hand. They worked well together. Joslyn had been faxing sections of the report to Chad while he was still on-site. He, in turn, would read them after the fieldwork was done, and return comments and edits by fax. So, the report was well on its way to being ready for the peer review required by the institute for all scientific reports.

In thinking back on the study, Chad felt good about the results and his findings. The extensive canal diversions of water from the Everglades took its toll on the ecology of those wetlands. In drought years, the severity of the impact was magnified. Chad wondered what the institute was going to do with the results of the study and his recommendations that many of the canals should be reverted to open wetlands. Certainly, the example of the restoration work being done on the Kissimmee River would provide insights of the value and costs of a management decision that would affect both the socioeconomic status of the region and the ecology of this fragile ecosystem. The Kissimmee River is a major watershed that drains the area around Orlando, Florida, and feeds the Everglades with much-needed water and nutrients. Its canalization by the Corp of Engineers in the 1940's had altered significantly the drainage pattern to the Everglades. Its newly initiated restoration had been a heatedly debated issue, and a major coup for environmentalists.

The only downside to Chad's field trip had been his encounter with the drug runners. It was apparent that the Everglades serve as a refuge for more than wildlife. Through his and Red's assistance to the DEA following their encounter in the 'Glades, a major drug cartel had been disbanded, and key leaders put under arrest. Chad and Red were able to show the DEA the areas where the drug transactions took place, and important papers linking business executives to the lucrative drug trade were found in the brief cases in the airboat of the drug runners. Red, who had spent most of his life near the Everglades, was contracted by the DEA to provide continued service in transporting field officers on drug patrol throughout the numerous channels of the Everglades. Chad smiled when he thought of Red trying to take control over the operations of the DEA, as he had when working with Chad on the environmental study. He knew that the DEA would have their hands full, but would appreciate the extensive knowledge and common sense that Red had to offer.

The plane landed in Asheville, North Carolina, home of the Phoenix Environmental Research Institute, a non-profit semi-governmental environmental research center. Chad Gunnings had been employed by PERI for almost eight years and was a senior aquatic biologist with the firm. The mission of PERI or simply the Institute was to conduct environmental research on specific issues where the balance of ecosystem protection and socioeconomic concerns was in question. By virtue of this mission, most studies were quite contentious, and subject to extreme dissension among several interested parties. In situations where human activities, particularly landward expansions, countered common sense for environmental protection, confrontations could become volatile.

Little was known of who specifically controlled the overall mission and made the assignments of the Institute. It was relatively common knowledge that there was a semi-governmental connection to the Institute and its studies. Chad knew that Senator Tremain Hodges of North Carolina was the key contact between the Institute and the US government. Senator Hodges was born and bred a southerner. His speech, mannerism, and life style all bespoke a man from the Deep South. His features were vaguely reminiscent of the fictional Colonel Sanders of fried chicken fame. Senator Hodges interacted often with the management of the institute and its senior scientists, but he did not with the junior and support staff. One had to reach a certain rank to become part of the inner circle of the workings of the Institute. He only socialized with the support staff and did business with the senior scientists. However, even as part of the inner circle, there was much that was unknown to the scientists. Because the work was plentiful and the scientific staff who were the best in their field were given much latitude in publishing their scientific findings, as well as participating in the various scientific conferences, they were not concerned about the specific details of the management of the institute.

Senator Hodges would visit the institute often and hardly ever missed the monthly senior-level staff meeting. Together with the Institute Director, he would lay out the next studies or discuss work in progress. There never seemed to be concern for funding, and the scientists never questioned that aspect. They were just as happy to leave the questions of where the funding would come from to those in the institute who kept the necessary records. The institute never lacked for assignments, which were international in scope and took its scientific staff to the four corners of the Earth.

It was not clear where Senator Hodges got his instructions; or, whether he directed his own destiny and that of the Institute. He always seemed to know what was going on with the various Institute activities, and never lacked for new initiatives. His first item of business when arriving at the Institute was to meet behind closed doors with the director, Sir Thomas Hilary.

Sir Hilary was a misplaced British subject, somehow relegated to the mountains of North Carolina to head the Phoenix Environmental Research Institute. There was speculation that Sir

Hilary was still a citizen of Great Britain and that his periodic trips back to the mother country were for more than visiting family. No one was very clear on the background of his knighthood, which was a topic of discussion among staff at the institute -- when there was time to dwell on such matters.

Chad knew that Sir Hilary's scientific background was not as in-depth as that of his staff. However, Chad marveled at his ability to comprehend complex issues and offer insightful advice or guidance. He compared Sir Hilary and Senator Hodges in his mind. Sir Hilary's British accent was as pronounced as Senator Hodges' southern accent. Sir Hilary was also much taller than Senator Hodges and as thin as the Senator was heavy. Sir Hilary was an impeccable dresser, and Senator Hodges always looked somewhat unkempt in his rumpled suit. He thought the two of them looked as different as could be, and in a sense, made a very comical pair. However, he believed it was uncanny how compatible these two men were in their thinking.

Chad turned his jeep into the entrance to the institute waving at the guard as he passed the gate. The Institute maintained a full twenty four-hour security force that almost matched the scientific staff in numbers. He had been told the maximum security of the Institute was necessary for protection of the expensive equipment and priceless scientific data produced by the numerous studies. Chad did not question the seeming over extravagance of the situation, because funding seemed to be sufficient to support all the operations of the institute.

As he passed through the receptionist area on his way to his office, he was met by Meg Martin, the administrative assistant to the director. "Hi, Chad. It's good to see you again."

Chad felt the familiar ache in his stomach at seeing her infectious smile once again. They had been lovers briefly, but the demands of the job made a long-term relationship impossible. Sunlight slanted through the open window, catching her strawberry-blond hair. "It's good to see you too."

"You've been gone quite a while." Meg's blue/green eyes twinkled.

Chad shifted his gaze away from her. "Yeah, it's nice to be back."

Meg glanced at her appointment book. "Sir Hilary wants to see you pronto for a debriefing."

"That's quick – I just got back. Give me a moment to round up Joslyn and we'll both come to his office."

"Actually, he would like to see you immediately. Getting Joslyn won't be necessary." Meg's gaze fell on Chad. "If you're free, stop by tonight. I'll fix dinner and you can tell me about your trip."

"Okay, I'd love to. After weeks in the field, I would enjoy a good home-cooked meal. I wonder why Sir Hilary is anxious to see me now?"

"Well, he didn't say, but was adamant that he would rather see you now than later."

Chad walked down the hallway to Sir Hilary's office, wondering what could be so important that it couldn't wait until he had gotten himself situated back in his office and went through his pile of mail. He knocked on the door.

"Enter!" Sir Hilary called.

Chad opened the door and entered the spacious office with the dark walnut furniture that always looked recently polished. He always marveled at how Sir Hilary kept a neat office that was in contrast to the offices of most of his scientific staff. No piles of reports or papers could be seen anywhere in the office. Somehow, Sir Hilary was able to work on a multitude of issues and projects without having the clutter that others around him would have.

Chad was surprised to see Senator Hodges sitting in the office at the round table used by Sir Hilary for small conferences. They were both obviously expecting him. Their welcoming smiles suggested to him that whatever was on their minds did not involve any perceived problems with the Everglades study. The smiles also alleviated his fears that there might be some backlash from the time spent trying to help the authorities with the drug runners.

Sir Hilary offered him a cup of coffee, which he gratefully accepted. He was waiting for Sir Hilary to say something. But, it was Senator Hodges who spoke first.

"How was your trip, Dr. Gunnings?"

The Senator's formality never ceased to amaze Chad, especially with him.

"The scientific aspects of the trip went pretty well, all things considered, Senator. It was a good study, and I think you will appreciate the results." The coffee was rich tasting and smelled fresh. "I do apologize for the delay incurred by the incident with the drug runners."

"Now, don't y'all worry none about those bad men you helped to capture," The Senator drawled. "We're up-to-date on the whole situation, and have been in contact with the DEA." "You did a fine job, and the institute thanks you."

He only thought a quick moment about the Senator's statement that the 'Institute thanks him.' It seemed to him that a statement of that sort should have come from Sir Hilary, if it were to come at all. A quick glance at Sir Hilary indicated that he was not miffed at the Senator's statement. "Why, thank you, Senator. What kind of information do you need me to tell you about the study?"

Sir Hilary cleared his throat. "We do not really need to get a debriefing on the Everglades study, Chad. We actually called you in here on another matter."

As Sir Hilary was talking, he got up and walked to the electronic console on his desk and pushed a button. The curtains surrounding the large bay window began to close. Simultaneously, the two walnut bookcases at the end of the room moved backwards into a hidden recess and slid behind two other bookcases. Then a back-projection screen automatically moved forward to take the place of the bookcases. Chad immediately became more attentive, and a more somber atmosphere accompanied the activation of the secret projection system.

"When was the last time y'all were in the fine state of Alaska, Dr. Gunnings?" The Senator asked. As he spoke, the map of Alaska flashed up on the screen.

"Well, let's see. I believe it's been about 2 years. I was there to assist the University of Alaska with a study on the watersheds in the Talkeetna Mountains."

Sir Hilary stood and walked toward the illuminated map. "Do you remember the purpose of that study?"

"It was an environmental study of the effects of placer mining on the ecology of the streams in the area," Chad replied, watching Sir Hilary attentively.

"Yes, we remember very well," said the Senator. "But please refresh my memory of the meaning of placer mining."

"Sure," Chad said. "Gold washes down from eroding mountain rock and mixes with the substrate in the streams and becomes what they call placer. Placer gold can be in pebbles or boulders, or anything in-between. The placer mining technique is very destructive to the aquatic habitat, because the machinery essentially scoops up the gravel substrate in the stream and dumps it out the back end after the gold has been separated from the gravel."

Sir Hilary said, "Your research was complicated by the lack of cooperation by the mining interests and the local people who depended on the income from the mining for their survival."

"I remember that it was one of the most dangerous environmental studies I have ever conducted," Chad shuddered. "I lost two very good friends and colleagues from the hostilities encountered in trying to conduct the studies -- and almost didn't survive myself."

Chad noted Sir Hilary deep in contemplation. Finally, Sir Hilary explained. "We have been asked to conduct a study of the Kenai (pronounced Keen eye) River and its watershed." The map of Alaska rotated slightly to provide a more North/South orientation. Then, the animated map continued its rotation, and the Kenai Peninsula in southwest Alaska exploded from its association with the rest of the map. The Peninsula became more prominent on the screen as the rest of the state faded away. It was as if you were flying overhead and watching the changes in land form as you soared over the peninsula. The snow-covered glaciers in the east that were the Harding Icefield came into view, then quickly disappeared from sight to give a birds-eye view of the Kenai River watershed with Slikok Lake at its headwaters. The graphical display was impressive, and Chad wondered why this much effort was put into illustrating a simple map.

Sir Hilary continued, "The Kenai River is one of three major river systems that drain into Cook Inlet. The Kenai River is in the peninsula, and the other two are north of the peninsula. The Kenai River is important for the annual summer salmon runs, particularly for the King and Silver salmon. As a result, the Kenai River is important to both commercial and recreational fishermen. But, there is evidence that the spawning runs are being affected by the increased urban encroachment and the logging activities in the upper reaches of the watershed. A group of citizens with a strong environmental interest, called the Kenai River Protectors, have organized meetings to educate the public and to obtain support to close down the logging operations, and put restrictions on urban development. Apparently, some of the charter fishing companies are providing financial support to the Protectors as well as inciting hostilities among the members. They want an ecological study done to link the problems they are seeing in the river to the logging activities, which they feel are the primary reason the salmon fishery is suffering."

"It doesn't sound much like an objective research study to me," Chad said. "They already have their mind made up, and simply want the evidence."

"Yes," replied Sir Hilary. "But it is not as simple as that. The logging operations in the area all seem to be in compliance. In fact, logging is greatly curtailed from past years. There is some speculation that mines in remote areas of the watershed may be operating. It is only speculation, because there is no record on file for a mining operation in the area. This has not been confirmed, but is suggested in a short scientific report prepared a month ago by one of your colleagues." As he spoke, Sir Hilary produced a copy of a thin report from somewhere in the recesses of his desk and placed it in front of Chad.

The title of the report was, "Evidence of Catastrophic Environmental Effects in the Kenai River", and was authored by Dr. Katlyn Jones. 'Kat' Jones was a long-time friend of Chad's who had been a fellow graduate student. Chad's mind wandered to those times back in graduate school. They had shared the same life style with the typical university pressures, poverty level, and successes/failures that seem to link fellow sufferers together. It had been a year since Chad and Kat had last seen each other, but they kept in relatively frequent contact via e-mail.

Senator Hodges said, "As y'all know, Dr. Jones' article wasn't well received by the scientific community, because she couldn't verify the source of the environmental effects."

"I remember when that happened," said Chad. "Some claimed that her physical and chemical analyses were flawed, and that the environmental effects she reported were due to an unusually warm spring, which sped the thawing of the ice packs. This, in turn, increased the concentration of sequestered sediment and other pollutants in the river. Kat talked to me about the criticism she was receiving. She was quite upset."

"What did you tell her?" Sir Hilary asked.

"I told her that the criticism regarding her speculation on the cause of the effects was reasonable because she didn't have supporting evidence. I also told her that it was a good study and that it supported her original hypothesis. She just went too far and raised the hackles on some dissenting colleagues."

"We have reason to believe that Dr. Jones was right in her speculation," said Senator Hodges. "In fact, we believe that she was closer to the truth than even she realizes."

Chad's puzzled look brought a chuckle to the Senator. "The problem with y'all scientists is that you always have to have things as black and white. Y'all can't accept anything that might be a little gray. Well, that gray area is what we want y'all to investigate."

Chapter 3

The Farmhouse

Chad drove his jeep down the familiar lane, maneuvering around the ruts and bumps that can destroy suspension systems and jar teeth if one is not careful. The cherry blossoms in the orchard to the left of the lane were in bloom, and were illuminated by the twilight of the evening giving off a pinkish glow that was in stark contrast to the shadows of the other vegetation along the lane. This time of year was always beautiful in the mountains, with the flowers coming into bloom, the greenery starting to awaken as the winter recedes, and with a chill remaining in the air as the mountains make the transition between the winter cold and the summer warmth.

He could now see the farmhouse at the end of the lane with warm yellow lights coming from the windows on the ground floor. The scene was not unlike that from a Robert Kincaid painting where the profuse lights highlighted an otherwise serene setting. The view was inviting and familiar as he drove up to the house. It had been awhile since he'd been here. As he drove down the lane, numerous flashbacks of their times together ran through his mind. He remembered the leisurely times where they would lie side by side in the meadow talking and watching the clouds go by overhead.

Chad parked his jeep by the porch. Meg met him at the door as he walked up. They briefly hugged, and Meg gave him one of her infectious smiles that lit up her whole face. He loved to see her smile, and had been acutely aware that when they were breaking up her smiles were nonexistent. It had been her wish to break up, mostly because of his frequent travel and absences from home. However, it had been important to both of them that they remain friends, partly because of what they had become to each other, and partly because they still had to work together. The first two weeks after they had broken up were tough on both of them. Nobody at work knew that they had been seeing each other; so, while their co-workers detected a change in both of them, no one knew why. Thankfully, Chad had to leave for the Everglades, so distance and time helped both of them.

However, now standing here with Meg, he felt that old familiar twinge. She had changed from her green dress to tight jeans that fitted her long shapely legs and a loose-fitting white blouse with the top two buttons undone. He could not help but smile, looking into her blue/green eyes that had the old twinkle back, seeing her beautiful wavy, strawberry blond hair that was short and just extended beyond her jaw, and that smile...

"Hi, Chad. You're just in time."

"In time for what?"

"I have a roast in the oven, and I'm in the midst of making a salad. Could you please open the wine?" Meg was already turning back to the kitchen.

"Sure," replied Chad, as he bent over to pet Spike, Meg's black Labrador retriever. Spike had patiently waited for her turn to greet Chad. "Hi there, girl." Chad smiled as he remembered how funny it had been when they discovered that the dog was a female. Meg had never thought to check out the gender when she got Spike as a puppy. She had just assumed that Spike was a male. Chad had come over to the farmhouse a week later to see the puppy, and dutifully informed Meg that Spike was not all that she had seemed. They had laughed over the incident, and that was when they started dating. Spike was wagging her tail, furiously, as Chad gave her attention. "Hey, girl. Remember all of our walks through the woods? How about our swimming in the lake? Sure you do." He smiled at the dog's affectionate response.

Chad had thought his relationship with Meg would work, because she understood better than most women what was involved with his job. Meg certainly knew the demands of the job as a field biologist and also knew the dangers of the volatile situations to which he was exposed. But, perhaps it was just that they were not meant to have a long-term relationship.

As Chad walked to the counter, he remembered Meg's laughing at Spike's antics on their outings to the lake. The dog would get very impatient, waiting for these two humans to get their clothes off before entering the water. She would bark trying to get them in the lake to play.

He noted that the wine was a merlot from one of his favorite vineyards just outside of Adelaide, Australia. He and Meg had discovered the wine together.

"The roast really smells good. How did you have time to do a roast? We just talked this morning about having dinner together."

"I guess I just banked on your saying yes. Sir Hilary mentioned that you were coming in to work today, so I just set the timer on the oven, you know..." Meg blushed.

"But, what if I couldn't have come over?"

"Well, I guess Spike would have had a really good dinner tonight!"

They both laughed.

"At first I wasn't sure I wanted you to come over. When you left for the Everglades, I thought about you often, and wondered if I could ever feel comfortable working with you again. But, as the months passed, and the few times we talked on the phone when you called Sir Hilary, I felt more at ease with our relationship. I decided that the best thing for us was to have dinner together, as friends."

Chad gave Meg an appraising look, trying to think of the right thing to say. Before he could say anything, Meg changed the subject.

"So, tell me about your trip." Meg said taking a sip of her wine.

When they were dating, they would not discuss work. However, now it seemed alright, and Chad told Meg about his last trip. He described the more interesting parts of his adventure in the Everglades, including the experience with the drug runners. Meg was fascinated with the stories, and asked the right questions that showed her interest and stimulated more stories. However, she grimaced when he talked about the drug runners. Finally, she asked Chad if he was in town for a while or whether he had been assigned a new project.

"I guess I'll be going to Alaska in two weeks. Joslyn will be going with me," he replied.

"Oh," Meg said as she stared at her wine glass. "It seems like you scientists sorta check in at the institute, then are gone again. This is reminiscent of a discussion we had not so long ago." Meg fiddled with her glass.

"I know," Chad said. "I like to be outside, and I like to travel. This job suits me, as I said before."

"Yes, I guess it does." Meg sighed. "Sir Hilary and the Senator think an awful lot of you. If you want my opinion, I think they give you the harder assignments, or at least the ones where they anticipate some trouble."

"Meg, you must be imagining things," he argued. "I don't think I get any harder assignments than the others."

"Well, I don't like it much." Meg said, glancing into his eyes but not wanting to give him a direct look. "You just got done telling me about the drug runners and the snakes and alligators you ran into in the Everglades. How long is it going to be before you get badly hurt--or killed?"

Chad thought carefully about his response. "Meg, I am a scientist, and more specifically, a field biologist. The wilderness is oftentimes where I do my research. I happen to be quite experienced in the wilds and can take care of myself. Have you ever thought about the fact that it might be more dangerous for you to drive to work everyday than for me to take biological samples in the Everglades from an airboat? Running into the drug cartel was a coincidence and not related to our research."

He got up to open another bottle of wine.

"Chad," Meg sighed and turned her head to watch him.

31

"It's my position at PERI that allows me to be privy to some of the discussions that go on in Sir Hilary's office. After all, I am his administrative assistant. I suspected he was going to send you to Alaska. But, I wasn't sure." Meg leaned forward with a serious expression. "What I did hear was the Senator and Sir Hilary discussing the sensitive nature of this assignment. Someone with a high political profile might be involved. The Alaska wilderness is dangerous enough without complicating it with men who have a lot to lose from PERI's investigations. I hope you will be careful."

Chad sat there looking into his wine listening to the soft piano music that was playing in the background. His mind wandered to a similar discussion that he and Meg had when they broke up. He decided that this conversation was getting too deep, and he didn't want to ruin the ambience. He started humming to the background music and picked up his glass of wine. He clinked his glass against hers and grinned at Meg. She looked up and laughed. They raised their glasses to each other and drank. They continued with small talk about the farm, Spike, the beginning of spring — whatever came to mind. Soon, their thoughts were far away from Alaska.

Finally, Chad said, "let me help you clean up."

"Oh, no," replied Meg. "Tomorrow is Saturday, and I can do it in the morning. Let's just leave it and sit in the living room as we finish the wine." As she rose to leave the table, her chair caught on Spike who had been lying directly behind her chair. Spike was up in an instant, but not soon enough to prevent the chair from stopping, throwing Meg off balance. Having shared two bottles of wine didn't help her coordination. As she started to fall, Chad was there to catch her, having already risen from the table. It all happened so suddenly. He caught one of her outstretched arms, and his other hand closed around her waist. In an instant, he had her on her feet and pulled her to him.

Meg leaned against him and laid her head on his chest. He could feel her soft breasts against his chest. For a moment, they just held each other.

They released their embrace and gazed into each other's eyes. His eyes saddened as he spoke n a thick voice. "I should go. Tomorrow is a work day." He immediately regretted adding the old cliché.

"Yes, you probably should," Meg agreed.

He could not tell from her expression whether she was sad he was leaving or sad their relationship was never going to be as before. He guessed the latter.

As he walked to his jeep, she watched from the doorway. "Remember what I said," she called.

He stopped and turned, not sure of her reference.

"Be careful," she added and closed the door.

Chapter 4

Berkeley

The burly man peeked around the large oak tree to see who was coming down the well-manicured path on the campus of the University of California in Berkeley. With his blue and white flannel shirt, soiled coveralls, and scruffy beard, he looked very much out-of-place. His shifting eyes kept looking down the path, then he would pull back, and glance at another man positioned on the other side of the path by a smaller tree. The second man was nonchalantly leaning against a tree, not trying to be too obvious, yet not attempting to hide himself. His tree was down the path about eight meters from the position of the oak tree, where his partner fidgeted and waited. This second man was younger than the first and was well groomed. He could have passed easily for a graduate student.

It was twilight going on dark, and the lights were coming on around the campus. However, the lamppost nearest the two men remained dark — they had removed the halogen light earlier. Very few people were on this part of the campus at this time of the evening.

Kat exited from the main lecture hall on campus, accompanied by a distinguished-looking, older man. She brushed back her long blond hair, which reflected the light both from the setting sun and the lights along the path.

The man was speaking: "What an excellent seminar you gave on the environmental condition of Cook Inlet, Dr. Jones. I think you had every student and faculty member riveted to their seats when you were describing the predicted effects of sediment loads coming in from the major tributaries to Cook Inlet upon the migrating salmon and summer visits by the humpback whales.

"Well, thank you Dr. Ravens — I mean Victor. Although, I just told them what I firmly believed was the truth. I guess my interest in the environmental health of the Alaska river systems has gotten a little personal, which is why I gave a passionate talk." Dr. Katlyn Jones was glowing with the praise from her mentor and boss, the Department Chair of the Entomology Department, Professor Victor Ravens.

"Passionate, I must say," exclaimed Victor. "It was definitely the most passionate talk I have heard you give. I can see that when you become involved in an issue, your whole lecturing style changes. I am duly impressed."

"Yes, I guess that is true," replied Kat. "I guess I never thought of it that way before, and..." Kat sensed rather than knew that something was wrong. She continued talking, trying to decipher her inner most trepidations that something was about to happen. If she could just figure what had given her a jolt to her uncanny sixth sense. "...and I am definitely able to be more persuasive on subjects of which I have a strong interest."

Victor continued talking. "I think you should give this same talk to the whole student body during the award ceremony for our Dean, Dr. Rogers..."

Dr. Ravens was interrupted by a young man stepping away from the tree. "Dr. Jones, aren't you the scientist who has been studying the decline in the salmon populations in the Kenai Peninsula?"

"Yes, I am," Kat replied. She instinctively shifted her weight, as she had learned in Kaju-Kenpo.

As the man approached them, he kept talking and smiling in a disarming manner, but moved a little to Kat's left. Following her instincts against directly facing the man, Kat turned slightly to the right while following the man with her eyes. Dr. Ravens entered the conversation. "Yes, Dr. Jones was just explaining her theory to the faculty and graduate students of the Entomology Department. She gave a very persuasive argument of the cause of the excess sediment loads in the Kenai River and its effects on the Cook Inlet ecosystem."

As Dr. Ravens was giving his enthusiastic account of the lecture, the burly man was creeping up behind them. Kat could see the movement out of the corner of her eyes, although she could not discern exactly who this person might be.

The man in front of them shifted his eyes slightly to the man behind them.

The man in front changed his tone. "I have been sent to give you a message, Dr. Jones. My boss wants you to quit causing trouble with your research. We don't need anyone coming up to the Kenai from down here to tell us we have problems." The man pointed his finger at Kat.

"Who is your boss?" Kat asked as she moved to the side, pushing Dr. Ravens off the path and putting herself in a position to see both men.

As Ravens was pushed off balance, he blustered, "What the..."

Seeing Kat assume a fighting stance made the men even more

wary. The burly man stopped where he was, and the smaller one held up both hands. "Now, Dr. Jones, this doesn't have to get ugly--especially if you take our advice and stay away from the Kenai."

"What makes you think I'm going to the Kenai?" Kat asked, confused as to why these two men had come all the way from the Kenai Peninsula to confront her on the Berkeley Campus.

"Too many people are interested in the Kenai now. It's none of their business. He doesn't want you to come back to stir things up again. We are here to deliver the message." As if on cue, the burly man stepped closer to Kat.

Kat quickly executed a back kick with her right leg to the burly man who was now upon her. As she made contact with the man's gut, she gave out a guttural 'ki-aye', which startled Dr. Ravens, but helped to center her chi, or internal energy. She immediately switched to a hooking kick with the same leg that caught the man in the face and knocked him sprawling. Without hesitation, Kat threw her force into a front kick, directed toward the young man in front of them. She caught him in the throat as he was beginning to throw a punch at her. She then switched to a side kick to the head of the man, which also sent him flying to the ground in an uncoordinated fall. In a matter of seconds, Kat had executed four kicks with only one leg and had knocked down two men. She then assumed the ready stance, as Victor looked on in awe and disbelief.

Both men rolled away from those dangerous legs, got up, and ran away in opposite directions.

"Wha-, wha-, what is going on?" Victor stammered.

"I don't really know," replied Kat, as she breathed deeply to re-center her chi and regain her composure.

"Where did you learn all that karate stuff?" Victor asked in amazement.

"Well, its called Kaju-Kenpo, and I have been studying it for years. It's not karate; although it is similar in concept. It actually integrates both Japanese and Chinese styles in its art. Studying the martial arts was important to my mental and physical well-being as I was trying to get through college and graduate school."

"Well, whatever it is, it certainly is effective. I think that one guy must have weighed well over 200 pounds, wouldn't you say?" Dr. Ravens was still shaking after the encounter.

"I guess I didn't notice. All I know is that we were in danger, and I had to do something," replied Kat, who was trying to bring her breathing back to normal after the short but intense exertion. She was flushed and troubled over the incident.

"The man was saying something about being from Kenai and that your research was causing trouble. Do you know what he was talking about?" Victor asked while he brushed himself off, as if he had been actively involved in fighting off the men.

"Not exactly," said Kat, thoughtfully. "However, I should tell you that my research there was not without some confrontation. I made a few enemies among the lumber factions there in the peninsula. I never thought it was serious enough for them to follow me back home."

"We'd better figure this out." They were approaching the Entomology Department building. "Come into my office. We should call the campus police to report these two men, even though they will be long gone by now."

The entomology building where both Victor and Kat had their offices was an old brick building built circa 1920. However, the marble floors were still in good shape, even after thousands of students and faculty had trodden through the halls. As they entered the building, a young campus police officer was just leaving, having made his rounds through the building. Dr. Ravens stopped him and told him what had just happened. The young officer left hurriedly calling in the incident on the radio clipped to his shirt.

"Now, tell me about those confrontations you mentioned, but neglected to tell me before now." Dr. Ravens sat down in his overstuffed leather chair in the ancient office that was decorated as if these were still in the 1940's. In fact, the office had not been refurbished since then, when it was occupied by another professor.

"I'm not quite sure where to start," replied Kat. "I think the problems started when I was in one of the local taverns at the end of a very strenuous work week. I was explaining my theory, which was not very well developed at that time, to two members of my field team. I remember the bartender listening while he was washing glasses. He came up and asked if my research findings were going to close down the nearby logging camp. Now that I think about it, I believe he was concerned about the loss of economy if the camp closed down. You know how those people up there are solely dependent on limited options for making a living. At this point, protecting the environment is not one of those options. The salmon fishing is not a big part of the tourist industry in that part of the Kenai. Logging is the big economy there. I told him that it was only a theory of mine and that we had not gathered enough evidence to substantiate my findings. I also told him that it would probably require another trip up there to really sort out the problem. He left us then, and started talking to a couple of other guys at the end of the bar. I didn't give it another thought."

"Do you think that the bartender is behind this?" Victor asked.

"No, I can't imagine why..." Kat stopped short. "You know, I think one of the guys the bartender was talking to was the guy who stopped us on the way over here. In fact, I'm sure of it, now that I think about it. This guy kept glancing our way in the tavern that night, and watched us as we left. I thought perhaps he was more interested in the fact that a blond woman was in the company of a bunch of men. I was the only female in the tavern that night. I shrugged it off at the time."

"You know what this means, don't you?" Victor continued without waiting for an answer. "This means you hit upon something that really scared the locals up there. Whether you truly believe your own theory, this attempted retaliation means that those people are

41

going to take precautions to be sure you don't snoop around anymore."

"Maybe I could be way off base in my predictions, and the folks up there are just concerned about their jobs." Kat was thinking about this. "But, what if my theory is right, and what if the environmental changes are irreversible to the salmon population and are due to some unknown activities up there--and not to the logging operations? Don't you think that the people should know about it?"

"Come on, Kat. Do you really think that if they would send two guys all the way down here to scare you, that they wouldn't do it again? I think there is some big money behind this, and that you may have stumbled onto something."

Kat walked to the window and studied the streetlights shining on the yard in front of the building. "I think I should go back to the Kenai to follow up on this. I wonder if I missed something in my previous visit?"

"I am concerned that your life is in danger -- especially if you go back up there." Ravens was insistent.

"But, shouldn't I follow up on this issue? Perhaps the logging operations are not the real cause of the problem. Besides, I have been criticized by my colleagues for not substantiating my theory. Victor, I think I owe it to myself to get to the bottom of this. How dangerous can it really be? The citizen environmental groups, the salmon industry, and the logging companies have been fighting for years over these issues and, no one has been killed, that I know

42

of."

"Don't you see, Kat?" Victor stood and leaned over his desk, staring at her. "If you provide proof for your theory--and it is the lumber operations, then the lumber companies will be put into a serious economical situation. Regardless of their interest in the environment, the livelihood of the local people will be at stake." Victor studied her face. "Do you really think you could sort this out with another trip?"

"Well, maybe it's a moot point. I don't have any funding to make another trip. How can I possibly investigate this further?" Kat crossed her arms in despair.

Victor was thoughtful for a moment. "I don't like the idea of your going back up there. It's too dangerous. But, I'll help you if it's that important to you. I just want you to think about it. Is it wise for you to pack up and leave abruptly?"

"I think this may be extremely important," Kat replied.

They were silent for some time. Then, Victor asked, "What do you think you would need to continue your research, and how much time do you think you would need?"

"I don't really know. I think that if I could organize another field trip up there, and had some assistance, I could probably collect the necessary data in two months. But, this isn't possible, because I still have classes in session. My teaching load is pretty heavy this semester, and a lot of students are depending on me."

Ravens sighed. "I know someone who I think might be

willing to help fund an expedition. As for your classes, if you could organize your lectures and outline the syllabus for a substitute, I think I can make the necessary arrangements."

Kat was getting excited at the prospect. "It is just coming into spring in Alaska. I must get the field work in before the summer rains that begin in July. Also, the salmon run in late summer and bring the fishermen in hordes. I don't have much of a window for my survey."

Ravens sighed again and stood up. "You better get started on a study design and proposal. I will contact my friend to see about funding." With that, Victor turned his back to Kat and stared out the windows.

Kat hurried from the building thinking furiously about all she had to do, and trying to figure out what the appropriate study design would be. Her sixth sense escaped her for the moment, and she did not see the young man standing near the corner of the building watching her leave.

Chapter 5

Anchorage

The sun reflected off the snow-capped mountains and produced a glare almost too bright for Chad's eyes. He was looking over Joslyn curled up asleep in the window seat of the Boeing 737, straining to see if he could tell where they were by the outline of the mountains. He guessed they were now over the Fairweather Mountain Range in Southeastern Alaska. He could see what looked like the Brady Glacier emptying into the distinctive Taylor Bay off the Gulf of Alaska.

He looked again at Joslyn, and noted her athletic stature, dark skin, and shoulder-length black hair that was tied back in a ponytail. She was petite, yet sturdy enough for the grueling field work that normally accompanied their scientific expeditions. She was sound asleep. Chad smiled. Joslyn had the ability to fall asleep easily at anytime, anyplace. Sleeping on planes was not difficult for her. Chad, however, couldn't sleep on planes, because he could not get comfortable. Whether he was too tall, too restless, too light a sleeper, he didn't know. All he knew was that they had been twelve hours trying to get to Anchorage, and the time difference was going to take its toll, one way or the other. Joslyn seemed quite relaxed and comfortable; whereas, Chad was ready to get up and walk around a bit to stretch his legs.

Chad was grateful that Joslyn Brown had come to work for him at the institute. What she lacked in experience, she made up in her cool dependable nature in times of crises and emergency. Joslyn had taken to the field work immediately, as if she had been doing it for far beyond her twenty-three years. In a predicament, she had an uncanny ability to see the problem and offer alternative solutions. Joslyn was especially good at being able to take control for preparing the equipment for field trips, which allowed Chad the freedom to plan the study design and strategize on the itinerary.

The plane circled over Anchorage and made an approach for the landing. The Anchorage airport is the largest in Alaska, but is still small, by mainland standards. Chad could see the beautiful Chugach Mountains to the east as they came in for the landing. They circled over Turnagain Arm of the Cook Inlet and settled in for a relatively smooth landing.

Waiting to meet them at the gate was a friend and colleague of Chad's — Elice Morningside. Elice was a Research Associate in the Anthropology Department of the University of Alaska. She was a Klutna native who had become a prominent anthropologist and known for her research on ancient Alaskan native cultures. Chad had met her three years before when the institute was planning their biological survey in the Susitna River Basin. They had become good friends, particularly through the difficult times they endured together on that study.

"Hi, RedBeardPaleFace!" Elice cried, affectionately calling Chad by the name she had given him.

"Hi, BrightEyes. My, it's good to see you again." Chad, gave her a big kiss and hug.

Elice returned the hug, seemingly drawing every part of him into her. "I missed you too."

They forgot that they were blocking the ramp with their long embrace. "Come on, you two," Joslyn said. "You guys are stopping traffic. Let's at least move off to the side."

Chad and Elice started laughing, a little embarrassed as they noticed people staring at them. Again, Joslyn took the initiative. "Hi, you must be Dr. Morningside. I am Joslyn Brown — the secret behind Chad's success."

"Hi, Joslyn. I'm pleased to finally meet you. And, I can believe you are Chad's secret weapon. He certainly couldn't do an adequate job on his research without you — I am sure. Ha! Please call me Elice."

"It sure is a pleasure meeting you, Dr ... I mean Elice. I have heard so much about you from Chad, and from reading your scientific papers. Also, you are prettier than Chad had said."

"Well, thank you Joslyn." Elice then turned to Chad. "Does that mean you don't think I'm pretty?"

"No, I mean yes... I'm sure..." stammered Chad. Then seeing the smiles on Joslyn and Elice, he knew that he had been set up.

As Elice turned to go to the baggage claim area and still laughing, Chad watched her jet-black hair sway over her shoulders and rest lightly on her full breasts. Her well-shaped legs moved effortlessly across the tile floor. Chad sighed and followed Elice and Joslyn who were talking incessantly.

After Chad and Joslyn claimed their bags, Elice led them outside to her jeep. "All of your equipment arrived the day before yesterday. I didn't open the crates, and just stowed them in my lab," said Elice, as she searched for her jeep in the parking lot.

Upon leaving the terminal, the cool wind coming off the

Chugach Mountains hit them in the face. Joslyn shuddered and asked, "How long is this trip, again?"

Chad laughed. "Ah, come on, you'll get used to it. With a little luck, we'll be through before winter sets in."

Joslyn shuddered again. "I sure hope so. My Southern blood isn't going to be able to take too much cold. It might coagulate right up and stop flowing altogether," muttered Joslyn.

As they approached the jeep, Elice and Chad noticed two men standing nearby, watching their approach. The men were dark-complexioned with black hair — obviously native Americans. "Are they friends of yours?" Chad asked.

"No," replied Elice. "They are of the Warrior Society."

Chad noted their distinctive colorful leather vests with bear paw prints painted on them. Elice pursed her lips. "The Warrior Society are native Americans who are ex-military. The Society functions as an organized para-military faction, who claims their primary mission is to protect the tribal associations from unfair governmental regulations and mandates.

"How did they come to be?" Joslyn asked.

"They were organized to serve the people, and even with their para-military focus, were sanctioned by the tribal leaders throughout Canada and the northern US. Members of the Warrior Society are usually called into volatile situations that were on the verge of turning violent. They are well trained and usually use their expertise in isolated situations.

"Yes, now I remember what I had heard about them," Chad said while setting down the luggage he was carrying. "The Warrior Society were in a high-profile confrontation over native logging in Quebec, British Columbia, and Nova Scotia. In this situation, the Warrior Society protected the native logging operations in the face of governmental shutdown attempts. Members of the Society served as security guards during the logging and trucking.

"That's right," Elice said. "The Society became well-known for its courage and obstinance to governmental pressures. In the eyes of native associations, the Warrior Society was the elite protector of native rights."

The two men shifted their positions away from the parked cars and slowly approached the trio as they continued walking to the jeep. Both men wore jeans and plain T-shirts. Their long hair flowed freely. Chad was studying the mysterious insignia on the men's colorful vests. He moved slightly away from Elice to the left as Joslyn dropped a little behind. "We wish to talk to you," the bigger man said in a slow deliberate voice. "We have been sent to ask you to not go to the Kenai River with your scientific equipment."

"Who sent you, and why don't you want us to go?" Elice asked looking straight at the man.

Chad watched the second man.

"The Clan Mothers sent us," the first man replied. "It is dangerous to go to the Kenai. You should not go."

"But, we must go to the Kenai. We have a scientific research

50

project to conduct," Elice said. "Why would the clan mothers object to our scientific expedition? We mean no harm."

"You must not go. The Clan Mothers have spoken. Are you not one of us? Will you go against the Clan Mothers?" The first man inquired more angrily. The second man turned to face Chad.

Elice said, "But, I don't understand. What is dangerous about our going? Why do the Clan Mothers..." She moved to the right, causing the first man to turn toward her. This maneuver kept the two men from seeing each other while allowing Elice and Chad to see each other more directly.

"You must not go!" The first man shouted, cutting off Elice's statement as he jumped to a position to put him in a better position to everyone in sight.

When the first man shouted, the second man moved into action against Chad. However, Chad was a step ahead of him, and delivered two kicks in succession to the man, first in the midsection, then to the head. The man dropped and rolled, regaining his feet quickly. The man assumed a fighting stance that indicated he had martial arts training, as well. He then took the offensive, faking a jab, then quickly following with a reverse punch and a side kick. Chad backed as the sequence of moves came his way, and in quick succession parried each blow. As the man was slightly turned after the side kick, Chad moved to the side and gave a fierce back kick to the man's chest. He jumped in close to deliver two rapid punches to the man's face. Then, while the man was stunned, Chad performed a jump reverse hooking kick that knocked the man out.

The first man lunged toward Elice. However, Elice swiftly sidestepped, bringing her fist down hard on his head as he slipped past her.

Joslyn was confused by the swiftness of the attack, but managed to recover sufficiently to swing her leather briefcase into the man's mid-gut as he stumbled past Elice. He doubled over, but quickly recovered and snatched the briefcase from Joslyn. In a single movement, he brought the briefcase up and smacked the surprised Joslyn knocking her against the parked cars.

Elice did not hesitate and stepped into the fray, with a hard punch to the man's kidney. As the man slumped from the impact, she delivered a strong kick to the face, which dropped the man to the ground, groaning. She immediately followed through with her arm clipping his throat. The man went unconscious.

Chad looked quickly to the other fight at the moment Elice was executing a hand chop to the throat of the first man. Once he saw the first man was down, he shouted to Elice to get in the jeep. He helped Joslyn to her feet, and they threw their luggage in and jumped in the jeep.

Elice wasted no time in exiting the airport parking lot and headed into town toward the university. They did not talk until they were clear of the airport and on the highway. "Why is it that when I am with you, I always find myself in tough situations?" Elice inquired.

"I don't rightly know. But, you would have a dull life without a little excitement, wouldn't you?" Chad smiled.

Joslyn piped in with an alarmed voice. "Are you trying to tell me that this is normal? What have I gotten myself into? Why didn't you tell me?"

Elice grinned. "I could tell you stories about your boss, here."

"What... what stories?" Joslyn asked.

"Well, when I first met Chad, we had to raft down the surging, cold Susitna River following snowmelt to elude a couple of poachers we caught in the act of slaughtering a small caribou herd on Federal lands. Chad kept me going because I was distraught over the murder of my brother by those same poachers." Elice paused.

Chad said, "When we stumbled upon the poachers, gunfire broke out. Elice's brother, Chopak, shot one poacher before being shot himself. I shot a second man. A third poacher jumped me and managed to knock out my daylights. Elice clubbed him with a tree branch she had grabbed from the ground.

After Elice helped me come to, we noticed Chopak lying in a pool of blood. I had to drag Elice away from Chopak because the remaining poachers were starting to get closer."

Elice managed a smile. "I guess we have been friends ever since."

Before they could get into more stories, Chad said, "I wonder what that was all about in the parking lot? To bring in the Warrior

Society must mean that something big is happening on the Kenai Peninsula. What could it have to do with our study?"

"I am also concerned about the Warrior Society's involvement. I don't like being on the opposite side of my people." Echoing Joslyn's question, Elice asked, "What have you gotten me into?"

"How much do you know about this study, Elice?" Chad asked.

"Not much. The message I got was that the PERI was sending you up to do a study in the Peninsula and that I was supposed to help you. I jumped at the chance, because it meant we could work together again. However, I don't know why you need an anthropologist for a biological survey of the streams in the area. I didn't think to question that at the time."

Joslyn also demanded an answer. "Ya, what kind of study are we doing here? I thought it was also just a biological survey. I have never been to Alaska before, and thought this would be a neat trip. Is there more here that is going on than we realized?"

Chad took a deep breath, not knowing quite where to begin. "I certainly don't have all the answers, yet, particularly because we were confronted by a group of natives that shouldn't be concerned with our study. I don't think I know all the dangers here, but I can tell you why we are here."

Elice had slowed down, now that they were safely away from the airport, and they weren't being followed.

Chad continued his explanation of the study they were about to undertake. "You both know that the environmental condition of the Kenai watershed has been deteriorating over the past couple of years."

"What do you think caused the problem?" Joslyn asked.

"It was thought that urban development and isolated logging activities were to blame. The Cook Inlet Protectors have organized a movement to eliminate the logging activities and to control urban growth. They believe this will protect the important salmon fishery in the peninsula."

"So, what does this have to with you and PERI?" Elice asked.

"Our mission is to determine exactly what is causing the decline in the fishery and pinpoint the sources for correction. We suspect that there is more than just logging in the upper reaches of the watershed, but we don't know what. Senator Hodges, who is linked to PERI, suspects that whatever is going on the Kenai Peninsula has some Congressional ties. He is concerned because it is all so secretive, and the evidence is very slight, indeed."

Chad paused as he searched the road behind them. "Hence, our study was not well publicized. How the Warrior Society found out about this is a real mystery. I wonder if we should go back to the airport and question our 'friends'?"

"I don't think that is a good idea," Elice said. "You know we will get nothing from those men. Haven't you seen all the movies where the Indians never tell what they know? Its true, you know. They won't tell us. Besides, they are para-military and won't be as easy to combat the second time around. We took them by surprise, and they won't let that happen again."

"You're right, Elice," Chad said. "The guy I was fighting was very well-trained. If I hadn't gotten in the first two kicks, it might have turned out differently."

"Yes, and if Joslyn hadn't helped me, I would have been in real trouble."

"I was never so scared in my life," Joslyn said. "I don't know what came over me, but it was an automatic response. It really hurt when he hit me with my own briefcase."

Chad said, "I think you are going to have a bruise for a while. But, it should be alright."

"Thanks — that makes me feel a whole lot better." Joslyn grimaced.

"You still haven't answered my question, Chad," Elice persisted. "Why do you need an anthropologist on this study?"

"Well, you are very familiar with the Kenai Peninsula and its people. There are native burial grounds throughout the Kenai that could be important to our research. I was hoping you would be helpful, not only to guide us, but to enlist the help of some of the natives in the region."

"Doesn't that answer why the Warrior Society is apparently interested in this study?" Joslyn said.

"Not exactly," said Elice. "The Warrior Society is only brought in when the native associations need protection. I don't think that Chad is a threat to the natives, are you, Chad?"

"No. On the contrary, I was hoping to get them to help me. Do you think that the native associations think we are going to close down their fishery?"

"I can't see the connection. The fishery activities of the native associations are even beyond the easy intervention of the federal government. It would take an act of God to change that," said Elice.

"Yes, I suppose you are right," admitted Chad. "Just the same, we need to find out what's behind the dangers those men were telling us."

Elice pulled into the parking lot adjoining the Anthropology building. She led the way into her lab and showed Chad and Joslyn where the equipment had been put. Elice left them in the lab while she went to check her mail. Chad looked for a telephone while Joslyn began inspecting the equipment.

"Hi, Meg," said Chad. "How come you're acting as Sir Hilary's secretary and answering the phone?"

"Actually, I am running the place while Sir Hilary is gone," replied Meg.

"Oh. Where did he go?"

"I can't say for sure. I just know that he asked to watch the place until he got back. Senator Hodges just arrived a few minutes ago. Do you want to speak to him?" Meg asked.

"Sure, put him on. By the way, it's good to hear your voice. I'm sorry we didn't get much time together before I had to leave again. It was more hectic than I thought to get ready for this trip."

"It's probably best it happened that way," Meg replied. "You see, I have been seeing another guy off and on for some time. We met while you were in Florida. I had intended to tell you the night you were over at the farmhouse. But, one thing led to another, and I guess it became awkward. I hadn't meant to fall so easily into your arms.

"Oh, I see..."

"I suspect you do not. I really do care for you, but I need more than an occasional fling. I have decided to date this guy more seriously. He doesn't work for the institute and doesn't travel."

"What's his name?"

"It doesn't matter. I don't think you two will ever meet. I gotta go. I will get the Senator." Meg put him on hold.

"Well, hi there, Dr. Gunnings! How does it go?" The booming voice of Senator Hodges came over the telephone lines.

"It's hard to say, Senator. Does getting attacked in the airport parking lot by some Indians count?"

"What did ya say?" The Senator inquired, incredulously.

"Yes, we were confronted by two men from the Warrior

58

Society, who turned out to not be too friendly. Do you have some information I should have on this?"

"No," the Senator replied. "Even if the Indians were on the warpath, how could they have known y'all were coming?"

Chad asked, "Is there a connection between the natives being riled up and our study?"

"I don't know what that could be, unless it's related to thar' fishin' rights."

"We thought of that, but it doesn't make sense. Why would they bring in the Warrior Society?"

"I guess I don't know the answer to that, son. I can tell ya that y'all should be extra careful up there. We don't know the full extent of the activities in the region. And, remember, the gun-carrying laws up there are pretty loose. Anyone can be packing a side iron, ya know."

"Senator, is there anything else you should be telling me?" Chad inquired one last time.

"Dr. Gunnings, I believe that we have told y'all the facts we know. I can only caution y'all to be extra careful. I can also ask ya if y'all know a John Masserman? He is a state congressman up there from the Kenai."

"No, I don't know him. Should I? What does he have to do with me?"

"I didn't think y'all knew him. I don't rightly know any connection with y'all and your study. Just be wary of him and his dealings. He might have something to do with operations on the Kenai — and he might not. That's all I can tell ya at the moment. Keep in touch." With that, the Senator hung up before Chad could question him further.

Chad sighed, and thought, "What have I gotten myself into this time?"

Chapter 6

Sqilantnu

They had been at it for three days. The planning of the trip was almost complete. Joslyn was getting pretty good about getting around Anchorage to find miscellaneous equipment to round out their field gear. Elice and Chad were looking over a map of the Kenai

Peninsula overlaid with different colors to note forest lands from grasslands, urban centers, managed lands, and Native tribal lands and burial grounds. Elice had been pretty thorough in her research to identify historical sites where past archeological digs were located. Chad had thought that knowing this information could be useful to them in investigating the cause of environmental problems in the Kenai River watershed. The tribal associations were very protective of their burial grounds and historical sites. Therefore, little or no logging or mining activity should be occurring on these lands. These areas of the watershed would serve as reference areas for their biological surveys of the streams and rivers in the watershed.

The field crew would be kept to a minimum and consist of four people — Chad, Elice, Joslyn, and Jasper, a guide they contracted from the Kenaitze Dena'ina tribal association on the Peninsula. Jasper Redtail had worked with Elice in the past and would be valuable because of his intimate knowledge of the area.

Elice and Chad were working at Elice's kitchen table and Joslyn was cleaning up the supper dishes. "Elice, what can you tell me about this site you worked on here east of Slikok Lake?" Chad pointed on the map. "It looks pretty extensive."

Joslyn came over to the table, curious to see where Chad was pointing.

"That site is pretty important to our understanding the ancient tribal cultures in the area," Elice said as she looked closely at the position on the map. "This is the oldest known prehistoric site on the

Peninsula. About eight thousand years ago, people migrated into the narrow, glaciated river valley and found an abundance of food to sustain themselves. These earliest of peoples were mostly fishermen and thrived on the abundance of salmon in the Kenai and Russian Rivers. These people were the ancestors of the Kenaitze Dena'ina. A more recent village was found to be on top of the older one. This one is nearly one hundred years old." Elice tapped the map with her finger. "Indications are that these more recent people are from the same ancestral stock, but did not inhabit this area for a long period of time. Something happened to abruptly end this later village."

"What do you think it was?" Chad asked, stroking his beard and looking at the map as if the answer would materialize from such a scrutiny.

"We don't know what it was, but we call it the Kenai Catastrophe. The Dena'ina call this region of the Kenai the *Sqilantnu*, and are quite protective of this area. The Dena'ina are pretty particular about who ventures into the area."

Elice leaned back in her chair and continued. "This site is where I first met Jasper Redtail, one of the Elders of the Dena'ina. The Kenaitze Dena'ina are similar in culture to my own Klutna. Both tribes are of Athabaskan ancestry and probably originated from similar regions in the interior of Alaska. However, the Dena'ina have retained more of the old ways, the traditions of their ancestors.

Joslyn looked at Elice in amazement. "This must really have been exciting for you."

63

"To be able to participate in the dig at this site was quite an honor for me. I remember that Jasper was one of several men from the Dena'ina who were skeptical of my abilities and uncertain of whether they wanted to accept direction from me. I admit I was a little inexperienced to head up the archeological digs at this time. But, the University knew the importance of this site, and to have a new PhD anthropologist, who just happened to be a native Athabaskan was a news item."

"But, why would the Dena'ina be skeptical about you leading the dig?" Joslyn asked. "I would think they would have been glad to have 'one of their own' in charge."

"I can see the dilemma," Chad said. "Elice is one of the few Alaskan natives who has succeeded in pursuing a career as a scientist. This has got to be foreign to them. Also, Elice being a woman, and in command, probably didn't sit well with them. Most tribes are male-dominated except for Clan Mothers who hold a special place in directing tribal affairs. Elice certainly isn't a Clan Mother — she still has all her teeth." Chad laughed, teasing Elice.

"Very funny!" Elice shot Chad a look. "But you are right about why Jasper and the others were reluctant to acknowledge my authority. I remember the first time I met with the men to explain why the dig was important and what I was going to do on the site. I must have talked for an hour without any interruption. No one spoke. I could not tell from their stone-faces that anything was getting through to them. I had to concentrate on their eyes. I can remember my grandmother telling me that to understand what is in a man's heart and mind, you must understand what is in their eyes. I have found that white men will give away their feelings by more than their eyes, but Indians do not."

"So, are you saying we white men are less complicated than those of your own blood?" Chad asked.

Elice gave Chad a long, searching look. "I guess in some ways that is true. But, I kinda like being able to understand another's feelings without working so hard at it. I find that rather attractive."

Elice continued to relate her first meeting with Jasper. "After I had described to the men of the tribe what the dig was all about and what we hoped to accomplish, I told them that was all I had to say and asked if there were any questions. Without a word, they all rose and filed out of the room. I wasn't surprised at their silence but was disappointed. I didn't see who rose first, so I wasn't sure who the leader was. However, I saw in their eyes that they understood what I was saying. So, I was going to have to wait until the next day, or the next, to see what would happen.

"The research assistants with me looked extremely perplexed after what just happened. One of them stated the obvious — that the tribal men hadn't given us the permission we sought to dig on their sacred grounds. I replied that we had to wait. The men had to meet among themselves and perhaps with the Clan Mothers before they could give us an answer."

"Did you have to wait long?" Joslyn asked as she sat on the

edge of her seat. "That must have been hard."

"It didn't take as long as I thought to get an answer. Jasper came into our camp shortly after noon the next day. We sat by the fire ring to talk. I remember that he waited until all three of my assistants had gathered around. I was the only woman. My three assistants were male graduate students who had asked to come along — this was their first dig. Jasper introduced himself simply as Jasper and said that he had been chosen by the Elders to speak. He paused while he collected his thoughts and asked me if I was the leader of the dig. I guess he had to be sure that I was actually in charge and not just asked to talk because I was a Native. When I confirmed that I was the leader, he nodded his approval. He said it was good, because we were of the same blood. That meant a lot to me, because, until he said that, I wasn't sure they would accept me. He continued on to explain the importance of the land to his people. While I already knew that, I listened patiently. I felt that he knew that I knew, but it was important that he explained the history of his people. He told us that he would assist in the dig and protect us from harm. I didn't ask what he meant by that. I guess I just thought it was a patronizing way of saying that we were unfamiliar with his land, and it could be dangerous."

Joslyn was listening attentively. "Was it dangerous? I mean, did you find out what he was talking about?"

Elice thought for a moment. "I guess I did. I think that Jasper was testing me. About two weeks into the dig, Jasper and I were in camp. The others were at the dig site. I was cleaning some pottery we had uncovered the day before. Jasper was sitting there on a log repairing a leather sheath. I wasn't paying much attention, but he was apparently watching something in the woods. The next thing I knew, I looked up and saw a grizzly walk into camp, sniffing the air. I was closest to the bear, and when I turned to look at Jasper, he was calmly watching the bear while he continued working. I was very nervous seeing the bear walk into our camp. I wasn't sure whether the bear was curious, hungry, or intending on protecting his territory. I quickly looked around camp to see whether there was any food lying around that we had forgotten to take care of. But, it looked as if we had succeeded in putting everything in the bear bags, which were hanging from a cable we had strung between two tall trees a ways from the camp. I looked back at the bear, which was coming slowly toward me. He stopped about eight meters from me and looked at me, sniffing all the while. I had put down the pottery and picked up a hunting knife I had on the table. I don't think I really thought what I was going to do if the bear charged, but it was an automatic reaction to pick up any weapon I could find. Jasper continued to work with his sheath, shifting his eyes from me to the bear. We didn't speak. The bear came as close as the corner stake and rope holding down the tarp under which I was seated. The bear sniffed long at the rope and stake, then, much to my surprise, he urinated on the stake and lower part of the rope, turned and left the campsite. I was much too surprised, and relieved, to say anything. I guess I just turned around and picked up the piece of pottery. I glanced up and saw Jasper looking at me. He simply grunted his approval and continued working on his sheath. Although we didn't talk about it, I knew that the fact I hadn't panicked was a big deal with Jasper. I think that was my rite of passage in his eyes. He became much more respectful after that incident."

The TV in the background had been going the whole time they were talking. However, they had ignored it at the time. Just as Elice finished her story, Chad's attention was drawn to the TV by some news item that was going on. The TV newsman was saying, "Yes, and Congressman Masserman is going to talk about his plans to support the bill that essentially eliminates any logging activities on the Kenai, except from the Native associations themselves. Up until a few weeks ago, the congressman was supportive of logging and said that the economy of the area depended on it. However, after meeting with several tribal associations and visiting the area, he has had a change of heart. Here he comes now. Let's see if the Congressman will talk to us."

Chad could see the camera trying to keep up with the newsman as he intercepted Masserman coming out of the state building in Juneau. "Mr. Masserman, can you tell us why you have had a change of heart concerning your position on the open logging issue on the Kenai?"

Masserman cleared his throat and turned to the camera. "I don't know as I've had a change of heart. I believe that I am just clarifying my position with regard to logging being done by the Native associations in the area. They should have first rights to the lumber in the region."

"Mr. Masserman, why did you turn against the commercial logging companies?"

Masserman stopped and looked narrowly at the reporter. "I have not turned against the logging companies. I am re-directing their operations to other parts of Alaska."

"Like the Tongass National Forest?" the reporter asked.

"No." Masserman kept walking.

"Isn't it true, Mr. Masserman, that the native-run logging companies are not as well equipped to conduct environmentally sound management practices?"

"No."

The reporter followed up with another question. "But, what about the environmental groups who have insisted that no logging be done, at all."

"Well, I don't think the logging we are talking about will cause environmental damage. The Kenai Peninsula is a big area, and a few trees taken from here and there shouldn't be a problem. Now, if you will excuse me, I must be on my way." With that, the Congressman turned from the camera and left the scene.

In the background, they could hear the newsman trying to recap the Congressman's statements. Chad turned to Elice and asked, "Why doesn't Masserman acknowledge that there is more to logging than just taking trees? The building of road accesses, clearing of understory, and large-scale removal of trees from concentrated areas are all destructive if not done properly. Actually, the large logging companies are getting better at minimizing environmental damage in most areas. I am not sure the native loggers have learned that kind of technology, nor have the equipment."

"It is curious that Masserman is supportive of the tribal associations, now. I have never thought of him as being sensitive to tribal issues. Also, did you see the two men behind Masserman? Weren't they the ones from the Warrior Society who attacked us in the airport parking lot?" Elice inquired.

Joslyn shuddered. "You're right, Elice. I hadn't really noticed them until you said something. They seem to be with Masserman. I wonder why?"

Chad continued staring at the TV, and said, "When I talked to Senator Hodges several days ago, he asked me whether I knew Masserman. He also advised me to be careful. I suspect State Congressman Masserman will be an important player here."

The music had everyone dancing. One of the best blues bands in the area was playing at the Chef's Inn. The small dance floor in front of the band was likewise crowded. Chad, Elice, and Joslyn were all up front dancing almost every dance. The three of them had finished putting together the preliminary plan for their trip and were now out enjoying themselves.

It had been Chad's idea to go dancing, because they had been working hard for three straight days. The music changed to a slow dance. Joslyn turned to walk off the floor, but Chad grabbed her arm while also grabbing Elice's hand. "Come on — let's all keep dancing." So, the three of them danced, holding each other in a three-way embrace. People watched them, smiling at the spectacle — a white man with a red beard, and two beautiful women, one African American and the other a Native American — all having a good time.

After the song ended, the band announced they were taking a break. "You two want to leave?" Chad asked.

Elice answered him. "Yes, I guess you're right. We should go. But, I was having so much fun."

They left the Chef's Inn, got into Elice's jeep, and pulled out of the parking lot. As they left, two men who were standing outside watched them leave. One man was burly. The second man was smaller and younger. The second man said to the first, "We will need to get someone to keep an eye on these three. You and I must get back to Soldotna."

Chapter 7

The Wilderness

The eagle soared high above the landscape, gliding easily in the air currents. The sun shone brightly, casting the eagle's shadow along the ground. With its acute vision, it searched the ground for any slight movement that would indicate an unwary mouse or rabbit.

With a slight tilt of his wings, he shifted direction minimizing his expenditure of energy and gaining loft at the same time. He had been soaring for almost an hour, patiently searching, but finding nothing. His acute vision was not failing him. He could see the three people hiking along the crest of the hill. From his altitude, they looked as small as rabbits. However, he could see the leather piece holding the woman's long hair in a ponytail. In fact, he could make out the Aztec-looking design engraved into the soft leather. These people were clearly not food for the eagle, and their passage was scaring off game. With another tilt of his wings, he turned westward into the sun and away from the crest of the hill.

The woman was leading her two companions as they hiked at a quick pace along the hill crest. She moved easily enough, being an experienced backpacker. The woman liked to lead, when she knew the way, because she liked to be the first to encounter new things. She had always had this curious nature since she was a little girl. She had an acute sense of awareness that kept her in touch with her surroundings.

The young man behind her was breathing a little heavily, and was not very used to hiking and carrying a heavy pack. He was the least experienced of the trio and worked hard at just keeping up the pace. He concentrated on where he was going and was not too observant. He usually missed things like the beautiful wildflowers growing in the field and the eagle soaring over them.

The third person was a well-seasoned hiker in his forties, and did not have state-of-the-art equipment as the other two. This man was quiet and didn't speak much. He was simply known as Trapper. No one knew whether this was really his name. However, he was familiar with the wilderness and had an uncanny sense of direction. He always walked behind the others, which made him more aloof yet enabled him to survey his surroundings.

The three had good hiking form. They stayed together, but maintained a distance of about five meters between them. This allowed them more reaction time if they surprised a bear or moose, or if one of them had some trouble. Don, the man in the middle, concentrated on this "distance thing", which made it an all-consuming purpose. But, that was the way Don was. The others took it naturally, and made it a secondary purpose.

This was their second day on the trail. They were making good progress to their destination, which was the upper reaches of Killey River located south of Skilak Lake and north of Tustemena Lake in the Kenai National Wildlife Refuge. Killey River was a tributary to the Kenai River. It was mid-afternoon, and they should reach their destination by early evening. They hadn't stopped for lunch, but ate some energy bars they had packed for expedient meals. By late afternoon, they could see ominous looking clouds moving in from the east over the mountains. It was that time of year when rain was a commonplace event, and the sun never seemed to set.

The woman stopped briefly to survey the sky. Don came up beside the woman and looked at the sky as well. "What do you think,

Kat?"

"I think we will make it to the campsite." Kat said, brooding about the incoming storm. Then she started down the crest along a steep and narrow game trail.

Don sighed, shifted his pack, and followed her. Trapper simply glanced at the sky and continued without stopping.

At the bottom of the hill, they came to a small stream, about six meters wide and flowing rapidly over rocks in the streambed, which created an extensive riffle. Kat paused long enough to search the best crossing, then carefully picked her way across the stream, stepping or hopping from rock to rock. Don watched her long legs as she gracefully crossed the stream. Kat made it look easy enough. Kat reached the other side and turned to watch the others. Once Don started across, Kat could see that the weight of the pack on his back made it more difficult for him to maintain his balance on the slippery rocks. At the midway point, Don's foot slipped off a rock.

"Don't try to..." Kat's voice was drowned out by all of Don's splashing.

Don tried to scramble back on the rock. In so doing, he quickly lost any stable footing he had and fell headlong into the stream. The cold water made Don gasp and flounder to regain his footing. He awkwardly slipped and fumbled his way out of the stream to where Kat was standing. Don climbed onto the stream bank, totally drenched and the lower part of his backpack was soaked, as well.

Kat was more worried about the laptop computer Don had in his backpack, than about Don's welfare. She wasn't concerned about Don getting a little wet, but the computer was another story. Kat glanced at Trapper on the other side who watched Don's antics without an expression on his face — but, she did notice a twinkle in his eye.

"Let's check out the computer." Kat said, as if nothing else mattered.

"Okay," Don gasped. "I'm... I'm sure its not... wet. It's in the top of the pack... and in a plastic bag."

As Don began searching in his pack, he saw Trapper's feet out of the corner of his eye. Don looked up and demanded, "How did you get over here so fast?"

Trapper shrugged. "I just followed the path."

"What path?" Don demanded as he scanned the rocks in the stream.

Kat interrupted. "Pull out that computer, Don."

Don pulled out a white plastic bag and gingerly removed the computer case from the bag. He unzipped the padded case and opened the laptop. He pushed a button, and the computer whirred into action. "See, it's dry and functional." As the operating system's screen flashed into view, Don typed rapidly to pull up a program as a test. When he was satisfied the computer was functioning properly, he turned it off and started pulling several 'zip-lock' bags of stuff from his pack. "It was a really good idea you had, Trapper, to put everything in plastic bags inside the pack. Where did you learn that?"

"I learned that the first time I fell in the water as a boy," Trapper said.

Don inspected all of his possessions, which were neatly contained in an orderly fashion inside the plastic bags. His socks were in one bag, T-shirts in another, underwear in another, a sweater in a fourth bag, etc. Don thought to himself that his clothes were not only dry but well organized. He'd have to remember this technique of packing. He wondered if he should do this for packing suitcases, too -- or maybe his dresser drawers. Naw, that was going too far.

"As soon as you get your stuff back in your pack, we should get going." Kat was looking at the clouds forming in the sky. "We have a little ways to go to get to the campsite. It would be good if we can get camp set up before the storm hits."

They hoisted their packs on their backs and filed away from the stream, moving quickly. It took them an hour to get to the place Kat wanted to pitch camp. They could tell by the incoming storm that they didn't have much time to set up camp. Kat and Don pitched the tent and attached the vestibule for storing equipment, then proceeded with putting up a dining fly some distance from the tent. Meanwhile, Trapper located two tall trees about thirty meters from camp. He climbed one tree to about four meters and tied one end of a rope. He then climbed down and proceeded up the other tree to about the same distance. He pulled the rope taut and tied it off. After he climbed down from the second tree, he briefly surveyed the positioning of the rope, then returned to camp to help with the final touches to the dining fly.

The rain came then, as they were finishing. The wind and the rain beat into their campsite, rippling the nylon of the fly and tent.

Kat watched Trapper as he scrutinized the layout of the camp and nodded approvingly to no one in particular. She had selected a good place for the tent, protected from strong winds and facing the appropriate direction with the curved vestibule facing the wind. The tent was a good distance from the dining area where all of the food smells would be contained. All of this positioning of the camp was necessary to prevent the occasional bear from entering the tent looking for food. She thought about the fact that bears tend to avoid the human smell unless it is mixed with the aroma of foodstuff or other 'smellable' products, like toothpaste, deodorant, etc. For this reason, Trapper had strung a rope away from the camp, where they would hoist a 'bear bag' full of all 'smellables' for the night. This would allow them to sleep peacefully — one would hope. Kat was satisfied.

Don was starting to shiver from the cold. He was still wet from falling in the stream, and the rain and wind weren't helping any. Kat told him to put on his wool sweater while she got out the pack stove. They were having beef stroganoff tonight — the dehydrated backpack food special.

After they finished eating and cleaning up, they consolidated all of their smellables into one large bag. Trapper took the bear bag and a rope to the trees where he had tied the first rope. He tied the second rope around the neck of the bag and swung it high over the first rope near the middle between the two trees. The bag dangled high in the air. Keeping the second rope taut, he took the end of the rope and tied it to a third tree as high as he could reach.

That night, a grizzly did come into camp. The bear was in the dining area when Trapper noticed the intruder. Kat awoke to find Trapper looking out the screen at the bear. "Can you tell from here whether it's a male or female, Trapper?" she asked.

"It's a female. Can you see the cub near the wood line?" Trapper pointed at a dark shape on the edge of the woods.

"Oh, yes, I see it now," Kat said. "That cub makes the mother more dangerous."

The grizzly didn't find much more in the dining area than a lingering smell or two. She moved out into the open, and stood on her hind legs to sniff the air. She looked at the tent for what seemed to Kat to be a very long time. Then, the sow bear dropped to all fours and ambled out of the campsite, heading for the place where Trapper had hung the food. The cub scrambled after her.

Trapper looked at Kat. "Well, there's nothing we can do until morning. We'll check out the food then." Trapper then scrunched down into his sleeping bag and promptly went to sleep.

In the morning, when Kat and Trapper went to check on the food and other smellables that had been hoisted between the two trees, Don followed closely. Don was both disappointed that he had slept through the excitement and a little frightened that a bear had come into camp and he didn't know it.

The bear bag was intact. However, there were deep claw marks on both trees, and the ground beneath the bag was scuffed up. It was apparent that the grizzly had tried hard to get the food. It had been wise for Trapper to tie the rope to the bag on a third tree at a distance from the other two. The bear had not figured out the solution to getting the dangling bag of food. Trapper inspected the perimeter of the area to see where the bears had gone and to be sure they weren't nearby. Having satisfied himself that the bears had left, he returned to help retrieve the bag from its perch.

While Trapper cleaned up the breakfast dishes, Kat inspected their field gear, and Don prepared the computer for entering the scientific data they would be collecting. Don was the last one to complete his task. He had to modify a part of the program to accommodate the biological data.

They were to leave the campsite set up and hike to the river sites they were supposed to sample. The campsite would serve as their base camp for the next few days. When they had loaded the appropriate gear into their backpacks, which were much lighter without the camping gear, Kat led the way to the first site.

It took them a little less than an hour to get to the first site. Kat dropped her backpack on the riverbank and began walking upstream to inspect the site for the best place to sample. She found the place not too far from where she had left her pack. The site she selected had a diversity of different habitats where aquatic organisms could be found, such as cobble, submerged logs and vegetation along the shores, and sand.

Don took out an instrument that was used to measure water temperature, oxygen levels, and acidity. He recorded the data on a field sheet. Trapper used a global positioning system device to note the exact location of the site. Then he measured the velocity of the water movement down the river.

Kat used a collecting net to sample the organisms living in and on the habitats. She could tell from the animals she was collecting that this site had good water quality. She saw many different kinds of insect larvae that live the majority of their lives in streams and rivers.

Don was watching Kat. "What are those things crawling around in your sample?"

"Insects."

"Insects! They don't look like insects." Don wrinkled his nose.

"It isn't until they emerge from the water and transform into adult, winged forms, that these animals are generally recognized as insects. The more kinds of insects and other animals, such as snails and clams, which are found in a river or stream, the healthier the ecosystem. Certain kinds of aquatic organisms are rather sensitive to pollution and will leave or die when exposed to pollution. The absence of these animals is an indication of a problem with the water." Kat looked for these tell-tale signs, but was generally satisfied with the health of the system. She took copious notes in her field notebook that would later be transcribed into the computer.

After an hour and a half, they had completed their survey. "I want to sample a site further up the river." Kat said when they had packed up their gear.

The second site was located only about a twenty-minute hike from the first site. However, the underbrush was thick, and the walking was difficult. They followed the river course, so didn't require a well-defined trail. After a strenuous hike, they reached the second site and did their sampling. This took them to noon.

Don said to Kat and Trapper, "I think I will return to camp now. This will give me time to start entering the data we gathered from the first two sites. When you get back from the other collections today, I can enter those data tonight."

Kat thought for a moment. "I don't really like your going off alone. However, the trail from the first site is pretty well marked, and you shouldn't get lost. The last site we want to do today is a pretty good hike. But, I think that Trapper and I can do that alright. Will you promise to watch where you are going and go straight back to camp?"

"Ya, okay. You don't have to worry about me. I'm not that much of a novice, am I?" Don looked anxiously at Kat, trying to read her expression.

Kat smiled. "No, I guess not. You're probably right in

wanting to get started on the data entry. We want to be sure we have it all recorded before returning to Soldotna. Okay, go ahead."

Don started out along the newly constructed path through the underbrush. The weeds and shrubs were still pretty high, making visibility difficult. However, Don could hear the sound of the river, even at times when he could not see it. He walked as fast as he could. He wanted to get back to camp to start entering the data.

Kat and Trapper finished packing their packs with the gear taking the instruments that Don left behind, so they could collect all the necessary data. Just as they donned their packs, they heard the distinctive growl of a grizzly and the unmistakable scream of Don. Trapper started running through the underbrush toward Don, yelling whatever he could think of and making as much noise as possible. Kat followed Trapper at an equally fast clip, also yelling.

Don had plowed through the underbrush to come upon a grizzly and her cub — perhaps the same one who visited their camp the night before. Don stopped abruptly, but not before the grizzly was startled by the seemingly bold intrusion and turned quickly to confront the intruder. The cub bawled and bolted away from his mother and Don. The grizzly growled, then charged Don. Don was already leaping sidewise and away from the grizzly. The grizzly swiped at Don's legs and caught his left leg just below the knee. Don's canvas hiking pants ripped as the claws gashed his leg. Don fell and rolled down the riverbank into the water. He landed face first, with the backpack sticking out of the water. The bear followed

Don and attacked his pack.

However, the bear stopped at the sound of the incessant yelling and screaming coming towards her. She looked around for the cub, bawled, and quickly climbed the bank and set off after the cub in a direction away from the noise coming through the underbrush.

Kat and Trapper found Don head down in the water. They quickly jumped into the water and pulled him up. Don coughed and spit water as he tried to recover his breathing. They pulled Don out of the water and on the river bank. Trapper took off his ripped backpack, noting that the laptop computer appeared to be okay. However, the cellular phone that Don was carrying for emergencies appeared to be damaged.

Kat ripped Don's pant leg away from the wound. The gash was bleeding profusely and had to be stopped. She held her hand on the wound and pressed hard, calling for Trapper to open the first aid kit and get out a compress. She then lifted her hand long enough to put the compress on and return to exerting pressure on the wound. Don started going into shock and Trapper covered him with a foil blanket they carried in their first aid kit for such emergencies. He then lifted Don's legs to help reduce the blood flow to the wound and increase the blood flow to the head. Kat continued the pressure for almost an hour to allow the blood to coagulate and stop flowing. She then put on antibiotic and wrapped the wound tightly in fresh gauze.

"Don has lost a lot of blood, Trapper. We have to get him out of here," Kat said.

"The cellular phone is damaged, so we can't call for help," Trapper said.

"Then we have no choice. He can't walk, so we will have to carry him. We have no time to lose. He will be getting a fever soon and may be delirious." Kat stood up to decide what to do next. "We have a two-day hike out of here. That may be too much for Don in his condition."

"I know a shortcut, but it won't be easy." Trapper looked into Kat's eyes to see if she were up to it.

Kat's eyes hardened with determination. "Let's get the camp taken down -- quickly."

Chapter 8

Masserman

"Hi, Meg. How is everything going?" Chad fumbled with the telephone cord.

"I'm fine, Chad. Work is uneventful. I have my garden planted — so I'm keeping busy. How is it going up there for you?"

"Well, we're about ready to depart for our survey. We have all the equipment ready and have gotten our supplies."

"Chad, I overheard the Senator and Sir Hilary talking about how dangerous this expedition might be. What's going on up there?" Chad could detect the concern in Meg's voice.

"We have had some trouble up here, but it's nothing I can't handle. You shouldn't be concerned about me. You have established another life for yourself and that should be foremost in your mind."

"You know that I can't just turn off my feelings for you overnight. We should be able to remain friends and treat each other as such, don't you think?" Meg was somewhat disturbed by Chad's insinuations.

"You are right, Meg, and I am sorry. I didn't mean to upset you. Anyway, don't worry about the danger. I will take care of myself – and Joslyn. Okay?"

"Okay. But you two be careful. I don't know what the Senator and Sir Hilary were talking about, but they were genuinely concerned."

"Meg, is the Senator there by any chance? I really need to talk to him."

"Why yes, he is. But, he's in a meeting with some of the other researchers. Let me tell him you are on the line." Meg didn't wait for an answer and put Chad on hold.

While Chad was on hold, he thought about how he had bungled his conversation with Meg. The last thing he wanted was to upset her. However, he guessed he was jealous that she was able to develop a relationship with someone else so quickly and that she really didn't want to see him except as friends. Chad had to shake himself, because this was exactly the same conversation he had had with himself before. Why can't he just accept things as they were?

His thoughts turned to the Senator. Chad knew Senator Hodges well. It was the Senator who had asked him to come to the Institute after completing his PhD. In fact, it was the Senator who had subsidized the last 2 years of his research to complete his degree. Chad had been on the brink of dropping out, because of lack of funding and mounting bills, when the Senator had come to him. Hodges had told him that Chad's major professor said he was a promising student who was contemplating dropping out of his program. The Senator told Chad that he had been looking for someone with certain qualities who deserved some help to complete his education. Chad had been reluctant at first, not understanding what qualities he had that others didn't, and he didn't want to be indebted to someone else. However, the Senator convinced him that it was not a free gift, and that he wanted him to work for a specific scientific institute when he had completed his degree. The Senator's jovial and somewhat patronizing attitude was disarming to cynics; it often resulted in his adversaries seriously underestimating his intelligence and recognizing too late that the Senator had once again outmaneuvered them. The Senator had researched Chad's background and knew of his martial arts training, which was one of the qualities that the Senator was searching for. Chad became quite enthusiastic over this arrangement, because it not only meant he could complete his degree, but he would have a job when he finished. Chad and the Senator became friends and were on a first-name basis during those early years. But, once the degree was official the Senator had always referred to Chad as Dr. Gunnings.

It was only a short time before he heard the booming voice of the Senator. "Dr. Gunnings, it's good to hear from you. What's up?"

"Senator, I wanted to ask you some more about Congressman Masserman." Chad paused to get a reaction from the Senator, but none came. Chad continued. "I saw the Congressman on TV a couple of nights ago. He has changed his stand on logging on the Kenai Peninsula. He now says that logging should be stopped except for the native operations. Why would he have a reversal of his position on the subject?"

Chad heard the Senator clear his throat before speaking. "There are those among us that feel that Masserman is in a difficult situation. It is true that he was pro-logging for economic development of the Kenai region. However, he's recently changed his position to be anti-logging, except for the Native associations. While this move was favorably received from the Native associations and to a certain extent from the environmentalists, he alienated the large logging companies and the people of the region who depend on the work. This position has put him in disfavor with his constituency. We think that he has ulterior motives for this peculiar change of events. It could be that he hopes to gain financially and this would provide some security for him in the most likely event he is ousted from office."

"Sir, to whom are you referring when you say 'we', and how do you know this?" Chad asked.

"Dr. Gunnings, I don't think it matters who the 'we' are. I haven't misled y'all over the years, so I ask y'all for your faith in this situation, as well. We only have suspicions about Masserman. No one has been able to get the full story from him."

"Senator, we are in the town of Kenai as we speak. Isn't that where Masserman has his office when he is not in Juneau?" Chad asked.

"Ya, as a matter of fact, he's there now," the Senator replied.

Chad was glad to hear that piece of news. "Can you arrange a meeting with him for me?"

"I guess I can. What do y'all hope to accomplish?" the Senator asked.

"I think that if I can talk to Masserman, I can get an idea of whose side he is really on. Besides, I have already met some of his bodyguards," Chad said.

"Y'all mean those Indians are his bodyguards?"

"I think so." Chad said. "I could see those same men who attacked us at the airport standing behind Masserman on TV. I want to find out what is going on before we get out in the wilderness."

"Well, then, y'all better be careful. Those Indians may not be so easy on you the next time around. I will see what I can do to set up an appointment. Hang tight, and I will get back to you. I want to talk to Hilary first, and he's still out of the country."

"Where is he?" Chad asked.

The Senator ignored his question. "Now, y'all take care." And, the phone went dead.

Chad and Elice walked up the long walk to the building set back from all the others on the street. As they approached the steps, they saw one of the men they had encountered at the airport and had seen on the TV. Elice glanced at Chad, but he kept looking straight ahead. As they approached the door, the man moved to block their way.

Chad calmly stated his business. "We have an appointment with the Congressman — Drs. Gunnings and Morningside." Chad paused to see the reaction.

The man moved aside, but did not open the door for them. He kept a stone-faced stare on them as they entered the office building.

Chad and Elice were met by a male secretary who took their names and asked them to take a seat. He then entered an inner office to announce their arrival.

It wasn't long before the man returned and asked them to enter the inner office.

As Chad entered, he immediately noted the second man of the

Warrior Society who had confronted he and Elice at the airport standing in the corner near the window. Chad looked at the man intently, and the warrior returned the look. Then, Chad turned his attention to Congressman Masserman who had not looked up from the papers on his desk. Chad and Elice walked up to the desk and waited for the Congressman to finish what he was doing.

The Congressman looked up and stood, greeting them with outstretched hands. He gave both Chad and Elice firm handshakes and smiled at them as if they were old friends. "Hello, I'm glad to meet you both. Senator Hodges said you would be stopping by. What can I do for you?" The Congressman motioned them to the leather chairs in front of his desk.

Chad wondered how much the Congressman already knew and what the Senator had told him. "Sir, as you know, I am with the Phoenix Environmental Research Institute." Chad saw the Congressman raise his eyebrows ever so slightly. I believe you are also aware that we are conducting an environmental study to determine if the present logging practices are adversely affecting the streams and tributaries to the Kenai River. The decline in the salmon fishery in this area has been associated with heavy sediment loads coming down the streams. We are here to discuss your position on environmental protection."

"What is it you want to know?" Masserman shifted in his seat.

"You aren't known for your support of environmental

regulation. You were always pro-development in the Kenai. However, it appears that you have spoken out against logging in spite of your previous advocacy. Why the change of heart?"

The Congressman shifted again. "I don't know why you think I have had a change of heart. I have always been concerned about the environment."

Elice spoke up for the first time since arriving. "Your voting record doesn't necessarily support that, sir."

"Well Dr. Morningside, I believe that I have made the right choice in my voting, given all the information on the issues at the time. Dr. Morningside, let me ask you a question. Aren't you in favor of improving Native rights? Don't you think that what I'm doing will help your people?"

"I don't know, sir," Elice replied. "You seem to have only recently taken up the cause of the natives. Also, it is peculiar that Native Americans of the Warrior Society would attack us, and they turn out to be your bodyguards. It seems to me, ah, us, that there is something about this situation you are not telling us."

"Are you trying to prevent us from conducting those environmental studies?" Chad demanded.

"That's a pretty strong statement. Why would you accuse me of trying to stop your study?"

Chad nodded toward the man standing in the corner. "Your bodyguards weren't too friendly at the airport in Anchorage when we arrived a few days ago. I want to know why we were jumped."

"I didn't direct these men to attack you. That would be kinda foolish, wouldn't it?" Masserman said. "Look you two, you are barking up the wrong tree. Let me assure you that I am not your enemy. However, with that being said, I would advise you not to conduct your study at this time."

"So, you are against our study. Are you afraid of our finding something out? Elice demanded.

"No, no, don't misunderstand me," Masserman said. "The loggers are real jumpy right now, and you might get hurt. That's all."

Chad made one last attempt at questioning the Congressman. "Where does the Warrior Society stand on these issues, and why are they with you?"

"Look, I think I've answered enough questions for one day. I have a meeting and you two should leave now." Congressman Masserman looked in the direction of the warrior who started toward them to escort Chad and Elice out.

"Don't bother." Chad stood quickly and extended his rigid hand toward the warrior with his fingers and thumb close together with his other hand parallel with his sternum. Chad had assumed a 'ready stance', an action that went unnoticed by the Congressman, but not by the warrior. Chad looked from the warrior to the Congressman. "We can show ourselves out."

Chad and Elice walked down the street. Chad brooded over the meeting. Elice looked at him and asked, "What are you thinking,

Chad?"

"It just doesn't make sense. In a way, we should be pleased that the Congressman wants to decrease the amount of logging going on in the Kenai. But, why is he mixed up with the Warrior Society, and what is it they want?"

Elice said, "Maybe he is telling the truth. Maybe he didn't send those men after us. Maybe we over reacted to the men at the airport."

"I don't think Masserman is telling us everything. And, I don't think we over reacted at the airport. I believe the men really did attack us. They certainly retaliated when we responded to their aggression. I just can't figure it out. Something is missing here." Chad frowned.

Elice slipped her arm in his. "Ah, come on. I don't remember seeing you so serious in awhile. Let's just not worry about it. I'm looking forward to this field trip. Let's go find Joslyn and see if she got the rest of the equipment." Elice looked at her watch. "We need to finish up here so tomorrow we can go see Jasper in the village."

Chad's spirits were lifted with the close proximity to Elice and her cheering attitude. "Yes, I think you are right. Perhaps Jasper will know something more that will help us."

John Masserman stroked his chin and watched from his window as the couple walked down the street.

Chapter 9

Soldotna

Dave Parsons was the sole police force of Soldotna. He had held this position for the last seven years. Before that, he was a fly-fishing guide. Fly-fishing was a passion of his, but it had gotten to be too much like work. It was enjoyable enough when his fishing party consisted of experienced, serious fly-fishers. It became work when the novices from the big cities came to experience a unique adventure. These novices were usually the rich, who had too much money and had trouble spending all of it. They came with too much equipment, sold to them by greedy salespeople who had no idea of what fishing in the Alaska wilderness was all about.

These 'novice' parties were definitely a pain. Dave had to do everything from carry more than his share of gear to actually catch fish, then he had to clean and cook the fish. Sometimes, he even had to de-bone the cooked fish for someone, usually one of the women who didn't want to dirty her freshly polished fingernails.

With the experienced fishermen, it was a different story. They caught lots of fish without assistance, cleaned and cooked their own fish, and shared generously with Dave. He quite often obtained a new recipe on these excursions. Yes, he enjoyed these excursions, even when he had to put up with the braggarts or the arrogant ones who seemed to know more about fish, than the fish themselves. However, the balance of the good trips with the bad trips had shifted dramatically those seven years ago. The massive advertisements of travel agencies had made it seem that the Alaska wilderness was accessible to anyone. The tourist trade was approaching that of oil in terms of importance to the Alaska economy.

Dave was cruising along Sterling Highway, which runs from the northern-most part of the Kenai Peninsula, south of Anchorage, to Homer and goes through Soldotna. Dave was in his early 40's, nearly bald but with a neatly trimmed silver-grey beard. His large, dark eyes twinkled as he waved to the people he passed on the streets. Dave was one of the friendliest individuals anyone would run across. He could talk to almost anyone about anything and always had a genuine interest in the conversation, which made him easy to talk to.

"Dave, are you there?" The dispatcher called over the radio. Dave shared the dispatcher with the State Police who covered Soldotna when Dave was not on duty.

"Ya, Helen, I'm here. I'm on Sterling Highway in front of Joe's Hardware."

"Jake called in from the Riverside Inn." Dave didn't have much use for the official police codes, and he enjoyed talking to Helen as a normal person. "He said that Fred and Bubb were back in town and that he was supposed to call you when he saw them."

"Are they at the Riverside House now, Helen?"

"Yes, Jake said that he waited for them to order drinks before he called. He wanted to be sure they were going to be there for a while."

"Thanks, Helen." Dave pulled over to the side of the road and then swung around in the direction from which he had come. After driving over the bridge to the Kenai River, he pulled into the parking lot of the Riverside House. The Riverside House was a well-established restaurant and bar in Soldotna. The side of the bar facing the river was a series of large windows. So, the bar patrons could watch the salmon go up the river during spawning season or the wildlife across the river in the brush. It was only a week ago that Dave sat in the bar having a beer and talking to Jake. It had been ten thirty PM and as light as day. They watched a cow moose trying to coax her two calves across the river. The water was moving too swiftly for the calves. They tried twice to cross the river, but the calves would be swept downstream, and they would struggle to regain the shore. After two attempts, the cow had decided it was futile and led her calves back into the brush. Meanwhile, just a few meters downstream was a small pond at the side of the river where a duck and her ducklings were being attacked by an eagle. The eagle would swoop down on the family of ducks, which dove under the water in a synchronized maneuver each time. After several attempts at trying to catch a duckling unawares, the eagle gave up. Jake and Dave had watched the whole thing and Dave had asked where else a body could sit and sip a cold beer while watching nature at its best.

Dave walked through the restaurant part into the bar. Jake was washing some beer glasses behind the bar. He saw Dave come in and nodded toward the table in the corner next to the window.

Dave was at their table before the men knew he was there. They had been talking quietly and drinking their beers.

"Hi Fred. Bubb. When did you get back in town?" Dave asked.

"Hi there, Officer Parsons," Fred said. "We've only been here for a couple of days. Mr. Parker sent us on some errands."

Bubb didn't say anything, just glared. Bubb was unsocial and always seemed to have the same clothes on — a plaid, flannel shirt and soiled coveralls. He took a sip of beer without wiping the beer foam from his black mustache. His beard didn't look too clean, either.

"You boys mind if I talk to you a bit?" Dave asked as he pulled up a chair.

Fred and Bubb just looked at him, waiting for Dave to talk.

Dave took off his hat and ran his hand over his balding head. He looked out the window and watched two seagulls fly over the river. Then he looked first at Bubb, and then at Fred. "I understand that there was a commotion over at Shirley's Bar on the other side of town about a month ago. I also understand that you two might know something about it."

Fred said, "I don't remember any commotion at Shirley's. Do you, Bubb?"

Bubb just grunted.

Dave shifted in his seat. "You don't remember Ray of the Dena'ina Tribe and his two brothers getting beaten up pretty bad? Witnesses said that there had been a lot of drinking that night and no one knew who started it. But, they said you two were there."

Fred said, "Well, now that you mention it, I do remember talking to Ray at Shirley's awhile back. You say Ray got beat up?"

"Ya, he was in pretty bad shape. He has a broken jaw and can't talk too well. He said he can't remember too much about that night, but did say you two started it. His two brothers were about as talkative as Ray. Now what's your story?"

Fred took a drink from his beer before answering. "Okay, okay. You know how Ray and those other Indians are always saying that they should be the only ones allowed to lumber this area and that they should be able to run their own operations. Well, Mr. Parker has done a good job running the lumbering activities for the Indians. Those Indians should be pleased. Bubb and I just pointed that out to Ray. And, before you know it, Ray and his brothers started throwing punches. It wasn't us who started it, Dave."

"So, you admit getting in a fight with them?" Dave asked.

"Well, I ... er, we ..." Fred stammered.

Dave said, "It seems as if the crux of the argument is the only thing you and Ray agree on. He has a different version of how the argument started. Listen, you two. I want you to stay away from the tribal members, or I will pursue this matter further. If I hear that you two are involved in another altercation, I'm going to keep you in jail and let the court decide what to do with you. I've told Ray and his brothers the same thing. Is that clear?"

"Yes, sir," Fred said. "You just keep Ray and those other Indians away from us."

Dave walked out into the bright sunshine and felt the cool breeze coming off the river. As he approached his police car, he heard Helen trying to reach him on the radio. He quickly reached through the open widow and grabbed the mic. "Yes, Helen, I'm here."

"Dave, we just got a call from Josh. He dropped a couple of fishermen off in his pontoon plane, and, on his way back, spotted two people hiking and dragging some sort of travois. It looks like someone may have gotten hurt and is being carried out. He circled them, and saw them waving to him, like there may be trouble. He tipped his wings to them and radioed in. He says they are about three miles from the Funny River Horse Trail. Can you take this one?" Helen asked.

"Yes, Helen, I can take it. I'm pretty close and will hike out from the trail. Can you call the rescue squad and have them stand by? I'll radio in when I reach them. I guess you know the rest."

"I know, I know. I'll have the State Police cover Soldotna while you are gone," Helen replied. "Good luck!"

This call was out of Dave's jurisdiction. But, Dave was probably the best qualified and experienced to check it out. It was not unusual for the State Police to call in Dave for help in finding lost hikers or leading a small task force into the wilderness for one thing or another.

Dave drove as far as he could on the Funny River Horse Trail. He got out and searched for the faint game trail. When he was satisfied he had found the right path, he opened the trunk of his police cruiser and looked over his gear. He wouldn't need his fishing gear this trip and moved it to the side. He always carried it in his trunk — just in case. He changed into his hiking boots, pulled out his day pack, the large first aid kit, two large water bottles, a flare gun, and his portable radio. As an afterthought, he put several candy bars in his pack. He had just bought a six-pack of Hershey bars this morning and had only eaten one, so far.

He called Helen on the portable radio to check whether it was working and to tell her where he was. Then, he fired a flare into the air, hoping that the hikers would see the flare and head for it. He put on his backpack and started out.

Kat and Trapper stopped to rest. They gently laid down the front end of the travois that they had been dragging. They had used a blanket to wrap around the poles that they had fabricated out of Aspen saplings at the place where Don had been mauled. Don moaned and shifted his position a little. The leather belt that Trapper had used to strap Don to the travois to keep him from slipping was chafing under Don's arms. Don was in an uneasy sleep, which was a futile attempt of his body to deal with the pain in his leg. Kat checked on Don, then took a long drink from her water bottle. She raised Don's head a little, bringing him half awake and helping him take a drink from the water bottle. She then lowered his head and splashed some water on her bandanna and wiped Don's forehead hoping to reduce his fever.

Trapper returned from scouting the path ahead. Kat asked, "How much farther do you think we have to go to reach the road?"

"I would say about two miles to the dirt road and another five miles to get out."

"Do you think the plane knew we were in trouble and will send help?" Kat asked.

"Probably." Trapper shrugged. "How is he?" Trapper nodded in Don's direction.

"He's got a fever and really needs to get to a doctor." Kat said. "Let's keep going. I hope that plane we saw knew we were in trouble."

They lifted up the two poles of the travois simultaneously and began dragging it down the path. As they looked toward the path, a flare burst upward into the sky ahead of them. "Look!" Kat pointed toward the bright light. "Someone's come for us."

Trapper had already seen the flare and noted its location on the horizon and the position of a rock outcrop and tall pine near the origin of the flare.

They were silent as they trudged for the next forty minutes. It was slow going, trying to keep the travois from bouncing as much as possible. As they came up a rise, they looked down into the valley. They saw a lone figure coming toward them. The man looked up at them -- and waved. Kat waved back, her spirits lifting as she saw him acknowledging their presence. She and Trapper continued on with their dragging the travois, trying to be careful not to jar Don too much.

When Dave looked up to see the hikers on the crest of the hill, he saw that one was a woman and that a third person was most likely in the travois. He couldn't tell how badly injured this person was from this distance. He would wait to use the radio until he could reach them and evaluate the situation.

It took another twenty minutes to reach the hikers. They were moving slowly because of the travois. Dave hailed the hikers. "Hello there! I'm Dave Parsons of the Soldotna Police Department. Is everyone all right?"

"Boy, are we sure glad to see you." Kat answered. "Don here was mauled by a bear." Kat said as she and Trapper set down the travois. "He's hurt pretty badly. We did the best we could."

Dave put down his backpack and checked Don's leg. The wounded man groaned when Dave checked the bandages. "It looks like you did a pretty good job with the leg. I don't think we should monkey with the dressing just now. Let's get him out and let the paramedics deal with it."

Dave pulled out his radio and called Helen. "Helen, I'm with the hikers now. Tell the paramedics we have a bear mauling on a man's leg. The man's okay, but needs attention. We are about two miles from the end of Funny River Horse Trail. I expect we should be there in about an hour. We will try to get there as quickly as possible."

Dave looked at Kat and Trapper. "How you two doing? Do you need anything — water?"

"No, we have enough water," Kat said.

"When was the last time you ate?" Dave asked.

"We had a little for breakfast, which, come to think of it, was

105

quite a while ago."

Dave passed candy bars to Kat and Trapper. "As soon as you are rested, we will get going. Tell me what you were doing up here, anyway."

As Kat munched on her candy bar, she replied, "I'm a research scientist doing a study on the tributaries to the Kenai River. We were out here doing some biological collections. We had a run-in with a grizzly and her cub. She attacked Don as he was returning to camp to do some computer work. We scared the bear off and started hiking out as soon as we could. All of that happened early this morning."

"I'd say you are pretty lucky. Usually, encounters with protective grizzly mothers aren't so satisfactory," Dave said. "If you two have enough energy, perhaps you could both pick up the front of this travois. I'll grab the back, and we'll turn this thing into a stretcher. I think we will be able to make better time. Let's go."

Chapter 10

The Dena'ina

The dusty road led through the entrance to the village guarded by intricately carved totems, past the gift and souvenir shop that was a major source of income to the village, past the lodge house where native dancing is performed for the tourists, and into the residential area of the village inhabitants. The road led by several wooden dogsleds in various stages of disrepair, children and dogs playing in the road itself as if it was the only playground, men sitting on porches resting after a day's work. The residential area was modest in appearance, cluttered yards, and seemingly, overpopulated. People stared as the jeep went by with an Athabaskan woman driving and a white man and black woman as passengers.

Elice drove down a side road and pulled up to an old hitching post in front of a log cabin. The cabin looked out of place in the community dominated by pre-fab houses. The cabin was old and probably predated the other houses. Curiously, the cabin was covered with bright hubcaps of all makes and styles. Chad and Joslyn stared at the scene, as Elice climbed out of the jeep and walked up to the door. As she approached the door, it opened and a man with wrinkled leathery skin and long graying hair stood there looking at her. His eyes swept over Elice and took in the other two in one swift second, then focused on Chad.

Elice said, "It's good to see you again, Jasper. You're looking well."

Jasper smiled with only his eyes. "It is good to see you also, Bright Eyes."

Chad wondered how Jasper knew that was Chad's pet name for Elice. But, it didn't take much imagination to look into Elice's eyes and understand the significance of that name, Chad admitted to himself.

"I have brought the friends I was telling you about," Elice said and nodded first at Chad. "Chad Gunnings is the research scientist in charge of this expedition. Joslyn Brown is his assistant. They are here from North Carolina." Elice moved back to allow Chad and Jasper to face each other.

Chad moved closer to Jasper and looked him in the eyes. "I have heard so much about you, Jasper. Elice regards you as a trustworthy friend."

Jasper looked at Chad. "What is an untrustworthy friend?"

Chad smiled. "You are right. A friend is a friend." Chad continued, "You already know that we are here to ask your assistance in an important expedition into the interior of the Kenai Peninsula. Will you help us?"

"I have already told Bright Eyes that I would help her," Jasper said. "I am ready to go whenever you are."

"Don't you want to know what we are doing and where we are going?" Joslyn asked.

Jasper smiled at Joslyn, showing his teeth. "Why would I ask of things I don't understand? I know you need my help to move through the wilderness. This I can do. What else do I need to know?"

Jasper, noting the look of exasperation on Joslyn's face, suggested, "Let's walk through the pine forest behind our village. We can talk there."

The four of them walked for nearly ten minutes without

conversation. An eagle soared overhead and screeched at the intrusion of the humans upon his hunting grounds. Jasper stopped and watched him for a full minute, then said, "My eagle brother warns us that our trip will be dangerous. There are those who don't want us to walk upon the lands."

Chad asked, "Jasper, has the Warrior Society been in your village?"

Jasper switched his eyes from the eagle to the cow moose standing in the wetland beyond the trees. "The Warrior Society is everywhere. They come. They go."

Elice looked at Jasper. "What did the Warrior Society want here? Did they meet with the Clan Mother and the Elders?"

"I met with the Warrior Society," Jasper said.

"Were they here to stop us from doing the biological survey of the rivers?" Elice asked.

"We talked about the land, the animals, the water. We talked about the trees and how they are being cut down by uncaring people," Jasper said.

"But, didn't they mention that we were here to help?" Elice asked.

Jasper thought for a moment. "They said that others from the outside were here to intrude upon the lands. They said this was our problem, not for outsiders."

"Then, why are you willing to help us?" Chad asked.

Jasper searched Chad's eyes, then said, "I believe that Bright

Eyes is a good person and is interested in my people."

"Then we must be honest with you and tell you that this will indeed be a dangerous venture," Elice said. "We don't know what or who we will encounter, but we are certain that someone wants to stop us. Men of the Warrior Society attacked us in Anchorage when Chad and Joslyn arrived. We don't know why. Do you?"

"They don't want outsiders involved in our affairs. They believe that his coming is bad for us." Jasper glanced at Chad. "I think they are wrong. However, if we fail, I may not be allowed back in the circle of the Elders."

"That is a lot of pressure on me, Jasper." Elice said. "I don't think I want to be responsible for your possibly losing your standing in the village."

"It is not your concern. It is mine." Jasper shrugged, as if he did not understand her concern.

"Then, we must begin immediately," Chad said. "We need you to lead us to the upper reaches of the Killey River, beyond Harvey Lake. We will approach where the Skilak Glacier drains down the valley. Will you do that?"

Jasper said, "I know the area. They are sacred grounds to which our ancestors migrated from the sea to start a new life. I will tell you a story." Jasper squatted down and looked off in the distance while he thought about the story. "In the days of the gold rush, my people, the Dena'ina, were driven from their homes by the sea into the wilderness by the white man. Men came from far away places to look for gold. Our old home by the sea became a place where ships came, and many men got off to search for gold in the rivers and streams. Soon, the white men outnumbered the Dena'ina, and even our new home in the mountains was not safe from the white man. The Dena'ina turned from fishing the sea to fishing the streams in the mountains and hunting moose and deer in the wilderness. But, the men kept coming. My ancestors tried to live in harmony with the white men. Some were good men. Others were not."

Jasper shifted positions and picked a weed absentmindedly, which he put between his teeth. Then, he continued. "One day, while the men of our village were out hunting, four white men -- prospectors -- came into our village. They were friendly at the beginning. They said all they wanted was to pan for gold in the stream next to the village. They asked two of the women to show them the places they could look for gold. The women led the men downstream from the village. When they were out of sight of the village, the men grabbed the women and ripped their buckskin dresses off them. The men then took turns raping the women. The women fought the best they could, but did not scream. The others in the village did not know what was going on. However, one of the boys of the village, who was about twelve years old at the time, had accompanied the hunting party and was coming ahead of the party to announce their arrival. From the cliff trail he was following, he saw what was going on below him. He quickly returned to the hunting party to tell the warriors. The warriors dropped their game and ran down the trail. They came upon the white men sitting around in a circle, with their backs to the two women who were dying from the cuts and bruises. The warriors killed the white men, but were not in time to save the women."

Chad, Elice, and Joslyn were silent while Jasper paused. Jasper took a breath, threw away the weed, and continued. "It didn't take long before more white men came and gathered up the people of the village and moved them off the stream and to a marsh area where many mosquitoes and very little game existed. The Dena'ina lived there for the next twenty years."

"Was that around the turn of the century?" Elice asked.

"Yes." Jasper studied Elice's face. "At that time, the United States Congress passed the Native Allotment Act, which enabled Natives to obtain legal title to one hundred and sixty-acre homesteads. Many were granted land on their old hunting grounds by the river through this Act. The people of the village then returned to their old lands in the wilderness. The village prospered there for many years. However, the village was mysteriously destroyed in a day at the time of the Festival of the Harvest Moon. Almost everyone in the village had left for the two-day festival, which was being held in another village some distance away. The only people left in the village were the old and sick, and a few others who stayed to care for those who stayed. When the festival was over and the rest of the people returned, they found the lodges burning and the people who they had left behind all dead." Jasper paused.

"That is what we call the Kenai Catastrophe," Elice said as she looked off in the distance.

"They never found out who had murdered their people. They did not stay there, but came back to the sea and to this village you see here." Jasper swept his arm to signify the village where he now lived. "The place where the village once was is the sacred place where you are going, and is called Sqilantnu. I will take you. We begin in the morning."

"Jasper, why didn't you tell me this story when I was researching the site before?" Elice demanded.

Jasper shrugged. "You were more interested in our old ancestors, not our recent ones. We do not tell many people this story. This is a matter for the Kenaitze Dena'ina — not for anyone else."

"But, why do you tell us now?" Chad asked. "And, why will you take us back there?"

Jasper looked off into the distance before answering. "I tell you this because you have been honest with me. I think we must not have secrets, because we must depend on each other in the wilderness. I also think the Dena'ina have gone long enough without knowing what happened to their people. I will lead you, because I want to know for myself — to find out what happened to my people."

Elice looked troubled. "Will the Warrior Society try to stop us?"

"I do not know." Jasper said.

Chad had been thinking about Jasper's story and the man's

personal interest in it. He also wondered at Jasper's willingness to go against the wishes of the Warrior Society and the other Elders. "Jasper, why is finding out the truth so important to you?"

Jasper looked into Chad's eyes and knew that he knew. "Because one of the women who was beaten and raped was my great grandmother, and the boy who alerted the warriors was my grandfather. My grandfather was killed in the Kenai Catastrophe."

Elice and Joslyn looked at Jasper in shock.

Chapter 11

The Riverside Inn

Dave sat at the table by the window in the Riverside Inn, watching Kat as she stared at the forest beyond the river. She was deep in thought. She hadn't touched her drink and seemed to be oblivious to Dave's presence.

They had been at the hospital most of the day while Don was being examined. His leg was broken — they had known that. He also had two fractured ribs and some internal damage, the extent of which was not yet determined. The doctors wanted to keep him under observation for a few days, and possibly longer, depending on the injury. Don had insisted that he be left alone but he would keep the computer.

Trapper had not gone into the hospital. He said that he did not like hospitals. Instead he took the cellular phone to see if it could be fixed and told Kat that he would return in a couple of days. He didn't much like cities either, although Soldotna could hardly be called a city. He would stay with a relative and couldn't be reached. Therefore, he would find Kat.

Kat was concerned about Don, but was very relieved they had gotten him to a hospital. She was now thinking about how she could continue with the survey without him. She and Trapper could probably do the survey okay. But, she didn't much like the idea. If anything happened to one of them, it would be very difficult for the other one to get the injured person out of the wilderness. Kat was brooding over her predicament, when Dave interrupted her thinking.

"Kat, you look very tired. You need some rest," Dave said.

"Oh, I'll be fine. I just need a hot shower and some food. I suppose I better find a place to stay before it gets too late," Kat replied.

Dave thought for a moment. "The only thing around

117

Soldotna is a few cabins that will be full of fishermen this time of year. Why don't you stay at my place? I have plenty of room — an extra bedroom, hot water, and food in the refrigerator."

Kat said, "Is your wife used to your bringing home strange women?"

"Oh, I'm not married and don't have a family — not even a dog. You will be all right with me. If not, you can call the police."

"But, you are the police!" Kat exclaimed, then saw Dave smiling.

"Ya, give me a call and I'll come to your rescue."

They both laughed at the thought. Kat wasn't very concerned. She could take care of herself, and she knew that Dave had no doubt about that.

While Dave and Kat sat there by the window nursing their drinks, Kat saw Jake, the bartender, watching them. She could picture Jake wondering where this policeman had found such a bedraggled woman. Jake probably knew everyone in and around Soldotna. Kat felt comfortable around Dave, and it didn't seem like they had just met. She thought about the fact that they had just met this morning and that through sharing a difficult trek and taking care of the injured hiker, that they had gotten to know each other quite well — sharing stressful situations does that sometimes.

As Dave and Kat left the Riverside Inn, Fred and Bubb slouched down in their truck. They had just driven up and saw Dave and Kat coming out of the Inn. They recognized Kat, immediately, and didn't want to tangle with her just now — especially because she had the police with her. When Dave and Kat had left the parking lot, Fred said, "Well, ain't that a fine fix we have here. I wonder how Parsons got hitched up to her. This will make things much tougher. We better get out to report this to Mr. Parker. He ain't gonna like this one bit."

Dave stoked the fire in the fireplace. The fire flared up into a beautiful mix of orange, yellow, and crimson. The fire crackled as the birch logs burned. The sound and smell of the fire quickly warmed the rustic, but cozy, cabin that he called home. He had closed all the drapes, which darkened the cabin considerably and allowed the firelight to illuminate the room. Kat opened the door to the bathroom, releasing trapped-in steam in the process from her long, hot shower. The action caused Dave to look up from the fire. There was something about Kat stepping out of the bathroom, dressed in his large, faded blue fleece robe, with long blond hair wet from the shower and backlit from the bright bathroom lights, that took his breath away. He quickly regained his composure, but not before she noticed his reaction. Kat continued brushing her hair as she came to the fire and plopped down on the overstuffed couch, folding her legs under her for added warmth. Dave moved away from the fire, which allowed the full effect of the fire's heat to reach her.

Dave went to the rough-hewn counter in the corner and

returned with two brandies. "How was your shower?" He asked as he handed Kat her brandy. As she reached for the brandy, her movement caused the overly large robe to fall slightly open. He could not help but see the gentle curve of her breasts.

"The shower was great! I can't remember when a shower felt so good." Kat smiled in genuine enthusiasm. It was true that she felt one hundred percent better having taken a hot, very relaxing shower. She also felt a little provocative, being dressed in nothing but the robe of a strange man she had just met earlier today. Kat was thoroughly relaxed. She was attracted to Dave, but didn't know why. They had just met, and yet they had quickly developed a rapport that seemed natural. She wondered about Dave and why he wasn't already married. She loved his soft brown eyes and his easy-going personality that he was able to transform into a take-charge persona when the need arose.

"You know, Dave, I don't know much about you." She said as he sat on the couch beside her. "Are you originally from here in Alaska? And, where is your family?"

Dave sipped his brandy. "Well, I've spent most of my adult life here. However, I was born and raised mostly in Michigan. I came here shortly after college, because I loved to fish and I heard the big ones run up here." He grinned, and continued. "I easily found a job as a fly-fishing guide, because I was good at it and had a genuine interest in people. It didn't take me long to locate the best fishing spots and to prioritize them in order of difficulty — you know, access

120

to the site, complexity of fishing strategy, remoteness, and so forth. That way, I could match up the particular trip with the experience and expertise of the clientele."

Dave paused as he sipped his brandy. Kat watched the flickering flames and sipped her brandy as she listened to his story. She sensed him watching her. She swept her blond hair behind her ear and felt it starting to dry from the heat of the fire. She turned her blue eyes on him and smiled. He returned the smile and took another sip of brandy.

Dave continued with his story. "I guess I never married because I was gone for long periods of time on these fishing trips. Or, maybe I just never met anyone. You know, there aren't a lot of possibilities up here. Anyway, it was only the last few years of guiding fishing parties that I was becoming less enthused about the job. The kind of clientele we were getting was not really of the outdoors type. I became more of a nursemaid and butler on these trips than a fishing guide. So, I took this job as police officer of Soldotna about seven years ago. And, here I am."

Dave stared at the fire for a moment, then looked at Kat. He shifted his position to turn toward her and rested his arm on the back of the couch, his wrist and hand hanging loosely near her shoulder. "Now, what about you? How did you get into this environmental business, and why aren't you married?"

Kat smiled and looked at her brandy as she swirled her glass. "I guess I've always wanted to be a scientist, and more specifically, a biologist. As a kid, I could always be found down by the creek. I love the sound of the water flowing over the rocks, the insects buzzing in the air, the squirrels rustling in the trees overhead, and the birds chirping and calling all around you. Even as a high school student, I hung around the local college biology department. I had a part-time job working for a professor who was studying bats. I remember one study where he wanted to see if newborn bats could be raised without their mother. So, he had me carry these bats around in pockets sewed to the underarms of a flannel shirt, and it was summer." They laughed.

She continued. "And, I would go out on dates wearing that hot shirt that hadn't been washed in a week. The boys would not know how to act around me. I guess the thought of someone carrying around baby bats under their arms was kinda weird."

The laughing subsided. They held hands. Kat continued. "I got caught up in the college life, the studies, and all the possibilities for a career. I stayed in school until I got my PhD, and went straight into teaching and continued doing research. I guess I never stopped long enough to have a meaningful relationship. I have had lots of friends, but nothing serious." She then realized they were still holding hands. She looked at him, intending to say something; but, nothing came out of her mouth. They just gazed at each other as the fire crackled and the light flickered upon their faces.

Dave tentatively leaned toward her to kiss her. Kat watched him, not sure how she would respond. As he got closer, she could sense his attraction for her.

Kat responded by tilting her head slightly and opening her mouth in demure encouragement.

Dave touched Kat's lips with his own — ever so gently, brushing her lips and she breathed deeply of his scent. He moved from her upper lip to her lower lip using the most sensitive touch with his lips.

She loved the sensation of his lips and soft beard upon her face and lips. She closed her eyes and allowed Dave to explore her lips, waiting patiently for his mouth to make full contact with hers. She hardly noticed as he took her glass from her and set it down on the table next to the couch.

Kat enveloped her arms around him, one hand on his neck to draw him nearer. She opened her eyes slightly and looked at him. The light from the fire flickered across his face, casting shadows that moved from one part of his face to another. She gently stroked his beard, feeling the softness.

Dave caressed her face, and they looked long into each other's eyes. He gently kissed her cheeks, nose, eyelids, and then her mouth once more. This kiss turned into subsequent, longer kisses, as the fire of passion grew. Dave led Kat into the bedroom. The embers in the fireplace glowed and dimly lit the cabin as the bedroom door closed.

Chapter 12

Johann Parker

Fred and Bubb drove at a higher speed than the rough road would allow. They bumped and jerked along the road as they raced along the dirt road that led to the lumber camp at Timberline Lake. The road turned downward, and they could see the compound of buildings surrounded by a tall chain link fence in front and the rock face of a mountain in back, from which the area for the compound had been cut. They finally reached a flat area where the road was well-traveled and less rough. They drove through a gate with a wooden archway and a sign that read, Parker's Timber Harvest. Two men in a log guardhouse recognized them and waved them through. Fred and Bubb drove past some outbuildings where there was a lot of activity of men and machinery. They drove up to a large ranch-style log cabin with a long covered porch that ran the full length of the cabin. Windows in the cabin were protected by the overhanging porch and were open to the cool summer air. Fred and Bubb parked the pick-up truck haphazardly in front of the cabin and walked quickly onto the porch and into the entryway of the cabin.

An elderly woman who was half Eskimo and half white met them at the door and blocked their way. "Now, Mr. Parker don't have time to fuss with you boys. So, slow down and go about your business -- but not here," she said.

"Now, Miss Elsie, we have something real important to talk to Mr. Parker about. I'm sure he will want to hear it," Fred pleaded with the woman.

"You boys never have anything important enough to take up Mr. Parker's time."

As Fred and Miss Elsie were arguing about whether the men would be granted an audience with Mr. Parker, a booming voice came from down the hall. "What's going on, Elsie? Who is that there?"

Johann Parker came into view. He was a large man with big hands. He was partially bald, and had a thick black beard with splotches of gray throughout. His flannel shirt and jeans were clean and of better quality than those of the men who worked for him.

Before Miss Elsie could answer, Fred blurted out, "It's just us, Mr. Parker — Fred and Bubb. We got some news about that scientist lady who is coming up here. We just wanted to tell you."

"What do you mean she is coming up here? You were supposed to take care of her. She wasn't supposed to even be in Alaska. You better come in here and tell me what happened." Mr. Parker turned and walked into his office.

Fred and Miss Elsie glared at each other as the two men gingerly stepped around her and followed Mr. Parker into the office.

Mr. Parker turned from the window and looked Fred directly in the eyes. "Now, you better tell me what's happening. Dr. Jones wasn't suppose to come up here. You were suppose to stop her in California." He clasped his hands behind his back and paced back and forth while Fred explained the situation.

Fred took a deep breath and told his story rapidly -- too rapidly. "Bubb and I tried to stop Dr. Jones in Berkeley. However, she had some guy with her who knew martial arts, and he was too tough." Fred didn't want to tell Parker that it was Kat who had the martial arts training. "Even with that, we didn't think that she would get funding to put together an expedition. When she did, we kept track of her. She was going in the wrong place when she started out, so we didn't worry about it. However, she and her crew ran into a bear who mauled one of the men with her. They came back into Soldotna and ran into Dave Parsons."

"So what does Parsons have to do with this?" Mr. Parker asked.

"Parsons is going out with her when she continues her expedition." Fred said.

Mr. Parker stopped his pacing and turned his back to Fred and Bubb to think about this new information. "I guess that does change things somewhat. We don't want Parsons snooping around here. Do you know where they're going to go?"

"No." Fred said. "We left as soon as we found out about them getting together. We thought you would like to know." Fred seemed pleased with his answer.

"You idiot!" Mr. Parker screamed. "We might lose them once they leave Soldotna. We need to know where they are going and if they are going to be a threat to us."

Fred, looking quite dismayed, responded, "I really thought you should know. I thought you might like to make some plans about them."

Mr. Parker was calm once more, and he thought for a moment. Then he said, "In the wilderness, anything can happen. It always does here in Alaska, and no one asks questions. I think we'll send a welcoming party to greet Dr. Jones and her friends."

Fred thought this might be a good time to give Mr. Parker the rest of the news. "When we were in Anchorage, we learned of a second expedition that's being put together by the university."

"What? What do you mean, a second expedition?" Mr. Parker again exploded.

Fred stammered, "Ya, yes. An archeologist there — I think her name was Morning- something or other..."

"You mean Dr. Elice Morningside, an Indian archeologist?" Mr. Parker asked.

"Yes. I think that is her name," Fred replied.

"Dr. Morningside led the expedition to the old village from the university to do an archeological dig a few years back. We watched her pretty carefully then, hoping she wouldn't turn up more than she should. She didn't," Mr. Parker said as he turned once more to the window, deep in thought. He turned around and said, "What else do you know?"

"Well, Dr. Morningside has a couple of people with her from somewhere else. I think it's an organization called the Phoenix Environmental something. I heard the name 'Chad.' They're planning an expedition to this area, as well."

Mr. Parker continued to stare out the window. "Tell me about this 'Chad.' What did he look like? Did he have a reddish beard? Was he tall and relatively slender?" Mr. Parker asked softly.

"Why, yes. That was him. Do you know him?" Fred asked.

"I don't know him personally, but have heard of him. If he is who I think, then he's Dr. Chad Gunnings of the Phoenix

Environmental Research Institute." Mr. Parker said. "When you said the Phoenix Environmental, I knew which group you were talking about. PERI, as it's called, is a global, international research institute. They have a record of becoming involved in controversial and politically tough situations regarding environmental issues. With the exposure and coverage in the newspapers on the salmon here on the Kenai, it doesn't surprise me."

"What does this all mean?" Fred asked.

"Let me ask you this question. Do Jones and Gunnings know the other is in the same area?" Mr. Parker asked.

"I don't really know. Do you know, Bubb?"

Bubb just grunted.

"I would wager that Gunnings doesn't know that Jones is also doing an expedition. Otherwise, they would most likely have coordinated and gone together," Mr. Parker said. "I think this will work to our advantage. We can cause an accident to both parties without their knowledge that they are both in the same area. It's important that we don't let them get together. We'll send welcoming parties to both groups."

"What do you want us to do, Mr. Parker?" Fred asked.

"I want you to take a couple of men and go to the old village. I'm sure that's where Dr. Morningside will be taking Gunnings. That area is avoided by the locals because of the superstitions surrounding the catastrophe that happened there some time ago. No one will be the wiser if an accident happens there. I will send someone to find

Jones and Parsons and bring them to me. I would like the opportunity of getting rid of Parsons, anyway. He's always been a thorn in my side." Parker grinned.

When Fred and Bubb left, Johann Parker walked out the back of the cabin to the rock face not far away. An entrance to a cave was somewhat camouflaged from being easily seen at a distance. It became relatively obvious as one got nearer to the rock face of the mountain. Johann Parker had been born and raised in Alaska and had inherited the logging company from his father, who had built it from a small operation. The lumber company had prospered in the early days, but had floundered a little under the increasing pressure from environmentalists to decrease timber harvest. Johann Parker had survived the rough times and, somehow managed to make the company a thriving entity once more.

When Parker's father died, the lumber company was floundering. Out of desperation, Johann convinced the local Native Associations that they should allow him to do the logging for them. By doing this, Parker increased the amount of land he could work by three-fold. The second thing he did was to restart his grandfather's small but discreet mining operation, which was not licensed in the state of Alaska. If Parker had licensed the mining activities, he would have been limited by environmental regulations that would hamper his making a profit. His grandfather had started mining at a time when regulations were pretty loose. However, his grandfather had encountered some difficulty when an Indian village appeared suddenly in his mining area. He tried many things to scare off the Indians. Finally, one day when most of the village was off to a celebration, Parker's grandfather rode into the village with several men. His intent was to pack up the village and send them out of the area. However, he encountered some resistance and had to kill two old men and three boys who had stayed behind. Parker's grandfather had no choice but to kill the rest of the inhabitants. Parker's father was a young boy then and had accompanied the men when they rode into the Indian village. He was appalled at the murders. When Parker's grandfather died, his father did not continue the mining. His father was still haunted in his dreams by the incident and only focused on the logging, which was legal. The whole business suffered greatly under his father's leadership. When Parker came of age to help with the business, he began to make it grow. Parker was aggressive with building the company, and became ruthless in the process, at the expense of many good people. Parker's father either turned the other way, or did not know all that went on under his son's authority. After his son became more involved, he had very little to do but to dream. His father's reoccurring dreams of the atrocious incident in his past soon caused his health to quickly deteriorate.

Because Parker thought the world of his father, he kept his actions secret from him. However, he justified his ruthless actions as a necessary piece of doing business in this wilderness. That unfortunate incident that happened nearly eighty years ago required the Parker Mining Company to maintain its secrecy. It would not do well for the Natives to learn of Johann Parker's history with the Kenai Catastrophe. Therefore, Parker went to great lengths to keep the mining as a secret operation ever since. Only his most trusted employees have had any involvement with the mining. With his father's death a few years back, Parker increased his mining activities, and now, mining is his primary passion.

Parker walked into the entrance that was well lit with lanterns. He walked deeper into the cave until he came to a fork in the passageway. He turned to the left and walked some distance to a series of rooms built off the passageway and into the rock. Parker entered the second door, which opened into a cavernous room. Metal shelves lined the wall holding numerous metal trays of pieces of ore. In the center was a long laboratory bench with various equipment for assaying the ore. An old man sat at the bench on a stool pouring over his notebooks and holding some ore in his hand. The man was entirely bald and quite pale, having spent most of his time in the cave. He was quite old. The old man had been called 'Judge' for years. He got the name, because when he made judgment of the quality of the ore, he banged an old gavel he kept by his side. If anyone knew his real name, it had been forgotten a long time ago. Perhaps the old man had forgotten, as well. It seemed that his whole purpose in life was to judge the quality of the ore collected by Parker and his men. The decision made by the Judge on whether the ore was good, potentially good, or bad, influenced Parker in re-directing the placer mining activities to search out the good deposits. The Judge used some unknown formula to determine the quality of the ore — it was some combination of the effort required to extract the placer gold from the substrate and ore and the purity of the gold. The ceremonious statement made by the Judge was never questioned by Parker or his men. The judge looked up as Parker walked in the room.

"Hello Judge," Parker said. "How's it going with the assays?"

In response to Parker's question, the Judge answered, "It's going well enough, I suppose, if I didn't get all of these interruptions." Parker was probably the only one to have visited the old man today.

Parker ignored the man's insolence. Next to Parker and his father before him, the Judge knew more about the company than any other man. He knew the mining operations were illegal, but his passion for scrutinizing small pieces of ore with the embedded gold and being able to predict whether subsequent mining was worthwhile, was too much of a challenge to pass up.

"I am going to postpone any further mining for a while." Parker said.

"But why?" The Judge asked. "We need to continue this placer gold sampling. I think we are about to find the origin of the gold we are picking up from the North Fork."

"Some strangers are nosing around. I don't want them seeing

things they shouldn't see. We just need to curtail our operations until they are gone," Parker said.

"Just ask them to leave. They have no business around here anyway," The Judge said. It seemed so simple to him — you just ask the strangers to leave.

"I plan to do just that," Parker replied. "But, until they leave, I think it best for us to hold up our activities. Besides, you could use a rest, old man. You haven't had a break in weeks."

"Don't you try to tell me my business. I know when I need a break and now is not the time. I have too much to do!"

"Now you listen to me, Judge. I'm the boss here and what I say goes! Do you understand?"

As Parker walked out of the room, he could hear the Judge grumbling to himself as he was cleaning up his mess. Parker smiled. The Judge was like a second father. But he sure was obstinate. Parker then turned his attention to the present situation — two survey parties invading his territory. He would have to do something about that.

Chapter 13

Chad's Expedition

The bumpy road tossed Chad around as the jeep hit each rock in the primitive road. Elice seemed intent upon maintaining a speed that accentuated every bump. Jasper was driving the second jeep and managed to keep up with Elice and Chad. Chad watched the second jeep through the reflection in the side mirror. He saw Joslyn riding in the passenger seat of Jasper's jeep, hanging on for dear life. However much she grimaced at the rough ride, she didn't complain.

Chad's thoughts shifted to the phone conversation he had had with Sir Hilary in the early hours before the trip had begun. Sir Hilary had encouraged him to move quickly in conducting the biological survey, but to be careful. He had told Chad that there was reason to believe that a man by the name of Parker was illegally mining in the area known as Sqilantnu, and that he was covering up his activities with a logging operation that he ran for the Dena'ina. Chad thought about what Sir Hilary had said about Parker being considered dangerous and that he was suspected of being involved in using physical force against the natives who opposed him. Chad knew that the biological survey that he was to conduct was on streams that ran through Sqilantnu and his survey would most certainly attract attention if detected by Parker and his men. Chad had asked Sir Hilary if he should recruit some 'physical' support himself for the expedition. Sir Hilary had advised against it, stating that it would be difficult to find a group of men who were neutral to Parker or who would fight against him should the need arise. Chad had asked Sir Hilary whether Masserman and the Warrior Society were associated with this Parker. Sir Hilary had not known, but thought that it was likely. If this was the case, it would be doubly dangerous — and there were only four of them.

Chad decided it would be best to move quickly, as Sir Hilary suggested, and to get out of the wilderness before Parker could know they were there. Chad had confided in Jasper so he would be able to lead them through Sqilantnu as quickly as possible. He didn't think it was a good idea to tell anymore than necessary, so only told Jasper the essential information and said nothing at all about it to Elice and Joslyn.

Soon, they came to the end of the road. Actually, the little-used lane they were on was blocked by a fallen tree. They would leave the jeeps here and backpack the rest of the way. They secured the jeeps, hoisted their fully loaded packs, and began the trek. Jasper led the way, and Chad brought up the rear.

The first night they camped on a knoll at the edge of some woods. After having stowed their food and other 'smellables' away from camp, they sat around a campfire that Jasper had going. It was that time of year when it stayed light throughout most of the night. Joslyn was talking about the beauty of the wilderness while Chad and Elice only half-listened. Jasper was carving a piece of wood near the fire. "It sure is beautiful out here," Joslyn remarked. "I can't get over how we can see so much at ten thirty at night. It's almost like noon with the brightness. Look at the tree line across the field. You can see the aspen and pine. And, look at the eagle flying over the trees. Over there — you can see..."

"Listen, do you hear that? Something big is coming near," Chad said as he listened intently.

"Sounds like a moose and calves," Jasper said without

turning.

Just then, a moose and her two calves came out from the trees and shrubs onto the knoll. Everyone sat perfectly still while the cow moose sniffed the air and looked around. She could smell the fire ever so faintly, because the slight breeze took the smoke in the opposite direction. The moose stepped closer to the campfire where the four people were grouped. The calves stayed close to their mother.

Elice said under her breath, "If we allow her to get too close, she will charge us. But, any sudden move now will probably make her charge, anyway."

Chad thought for a moment. "We need to distract her. When I give the word, Elice and Jasper — you move quickly off to the right. Joslyn and I will go to the left. Shout and wave your arms as you go. Now, go!" They all moved at the same time. The moose stopped short and swung her head from side to side, trying to see everyone at once. She snorted and started backing away. She looked for her calves, and when they were close to her, she turned and trotted for the woods. The calves followed closely.

"Whew! So much beauty in wildlife — we just don't need it in our camp," Joslyn exclaimed.

The next morning they started out early, though the sun was already high in the sky. They were in good spirits and talked as they hiked. It was late morning when they entered the area called Sqilantnu. Chad could tell from the change in Elice and Jasper's demeanor that something was different. They both became more quiet, and Jasper slowed his pace slightly. It seemed to Chad that there were fewer birds in the sky. The terrain became more rugged with cliffs extending above them as they hiked. They passed pictures carved into rock that depicted various shapes and sizes of humans and animals. Elice explained that these were not petroglyphs from the ancestral natives, but were most likely sixty to a hundred years old. The pictures were random and did not appear to depict any particular story. Some were huge and demon-like. Elice thought they were intended to scare off intruders.

They continued on through the morning, gazing at the pictures on the rock face as they passed. High above, a lone eagle soared. The path was very narrow and indistinguishable in places. Jasper seemed to know where he was going and led the way up the ravine. About noon, they came to the top of a ridge that ran some distance to the west. They walked along the ridgeline into the early afternoon sun. The wind picked up, which helped to keep the insects away from the hikers. Every so often they would see some furry creature streak out of sight across the loose rocks. Jasper eventually led them off the ridge and started winding down the mountainside. They entered the tall shrubs that littered the hillside. Jasper found his way easily through the thicket. They were careful to avoid the thorny devil's club that was sporadically growing among the shrubs.

As the hikers rounded a dense thicket of shrubs and trees, they startled a black bear feeding on a small patch of blueberries. The bear reared up on its hind feet and bawled at the intruders. The hikers stopped short. Jasper managed to produce a rattle, made of animal skin stretched taut over a small antler and filled with pebbles, from somewhere in his pack. He raised the rattle high above his head and began shaking it vigorously. It made a sound much like the sound a rattlesnake makes when threatened. The absence of rattlesnakes in Alaska did not seem to matter. The rattling sound was unusual and distracting to the bear. The bear stopped its growling and bawling at the urgent, high-pitched sound. The bear dropped to all four paws and backed away from the sound. When the bear was safely away, it turned and fled through the thicket.

Joslyn looked at Jasper. "Where did you learn that? There aren't any rattlesnakes here in this part of the country, are there?" she asked.

"No. But, this rattle is what we use in our bear dance and when we hunt the great bear. All the warriors have one, and we circle the bear and shake the rattles. The sound confuses the bear. While the bear is distracted, one warrior who is the designated hunter will kill the bear with his spear."

After making sure the bear had departed, they continued their trek. The trail was rough. Chad wondered how the people had moved an entire village down this path. He also wondered how they knew when they had found the right place for their village.

Late in the afternoon, they came to the old village where Jasper's ancestors had lived before the tragic massacre of nearly one hundred years ago. Elice described the lay out of the village and pointed out the area where the ancient village had once thrived. The ruins were not evident after so many years. However, they could visualize the village as Elice described where the various village structures had been.

They decided that they would camp where Elice's archeological expedition had camped while working the site. The fire rings were still intact and a path to the stream was still visible. They quickly went about their business of setting up camp. It was a relatively solemn activity out of respect for Jasper's ancestors.

The two Indian warriors watched the people set up camp from a cliff ledge high above the old village. They had been following the expedition at a distance all day, and knew the expedition would end up at the village. They watched as the dining fly was set up near the fire ring and the two tents erected farther away — the one for the women inside of the imaginary boundaries of their campsite and the one for the men closest to the outside. They watched as dinner was prepared, and the campfire turned to embers. The four people at the campsite were settling down for the night.

Then, the Indians turned their eyes to the distance where another camp was being set up. It looked like five men were setting up a fireless camp less than a mile away. The Indians said nothing, watched, and waited.

Chapter 14

Kat's Expedition

Kat awoke to the smell of coffee brewing and bacon frying on the stove. She lay there taking in her surroundings and feeling refreshed and relaxed. The bedroom was very masculine with Indian blankets hanging from the log walls instead of pictures and covering the old oak dresser and end table. All of the furniture was well-worn oak, but sturdy and tasteful — for a man's bedroom. Kat noted there were no closets but rather a large oak wardrobe. An ancient bamboo fishing rod with a rusty reel hung across the doorframe. She wondered about its significance.

She threw off the warm quilt and put on Dave's robe once more. Kat went outside the bedroom and leaned against the door jam to watch Dave at work in the kitchen.

Dave was busy tending the bacon and preparing the eggs. He was humming, oblivious of his audience. He poured himself some coffee, took a sip, and swore softly at himself for not thinking about the temperature of freshly brewed coffee.

Kat smiled at Dave's antics and walked into the kitchen. "Hello there, chef!"

"Well, good morning, gorgeous." Dave smiled broadly at seeing Kat standing there and looking so becoming in his robe with her tussled hair.

"You look like you slept fitfully," Dave said as he poured her coffee.

"Don't let it fool you," Kat said as she took the coffee mug. "Some guy kept waking me up periodically." She grinned.

Dave blushed at the memory. "I'm sorry," he stammered. "I just couldn't help myself. You were so enticing."

Kat rested her hand lightly on his arm. "I wasn't complaining."

They looked at each other for a long time. Then, Dave brought himself back to reality. "How would you like your eggs?"

"Over easy, please." Kat said.

"Okay, I was just wondering. You'll probably get them scrambled, anyway. I don't do real well on keeping the yolks unbroken."

"Scrambled is fine."

Dave concentrated on breaking the eggshell just right so the egg would plop onto the frying pan without damaging the yolk. The first egg came out just right, but the second one broke.

Kat laughed at the look of dismay on Dave's face as the second yolk broke. "You're batting .500, I'd say."

Dave grimaced. "Yah, well I still have to flip this one." He scrutinized the 'surviving' egg as it cooked, and scrambled the other one. He took a deep breath and flipped the egg, which immediately broke and spilled the yolk. He just sighed as he mixed it with the other to produce a fully scrambled egg breakfast. This made Kat laugh all the harder. She managed to blurt out a 'thank you' in between the laughter.

They had a leisurely breakfast and drank coffee while they talked.

Dave set his cup down and looked at Kat seriously. "You know, I have a few days of vacation coming. Why don't you let me come with you when you and Trapper go back out to the river? Don is laid up, and you need a third person."

"I can't ask you to do that," Kat said. In truth, she was torn — part of her wanted him there, and part of her wanted him to stay away. Maybe it was a fear of getting too close to someone who lived in a different world than she; or maybe it was a fear of destroying a promising relationship because of an intense work situation. Maybe it was a little of both.

"But, you are not *asking*. I am *offering*. Besides, I know this area pretty well."

"Trapper knows this area pretty well, too. We'll be okay." Kat argued back, but not too strongly.

"Okay, let me put it this way. You would benefit from a third person to help carry equipment. Plus, you would benefit from someone who knows the wilderness, and someone you can trust." Dave said.

"What makes you think I can trust you?"

Without cracking a smile, Dave replied, "Because I let you wear my robe." He knew he had won.

Dave started asking questions about the biological survey work she was doing, so he better understood what their mission was. They talked and drank coffee. Finally, Kat said that she should take a shower and get back to town to check up on Don and Trapper.

Dave started to clean up as Kat went to the bathroom to take her shower. Kat turned the water on about as hot as she could stand it. She knew that this was one of the last hot showers she was going to get for a while. She smiled as the hot water pelted her body and steamed up the bathroom, and she thought about last night. She had her eyes closed and didn't notice the bathroom door open and close softly. She felt the air temperature change slightly, more than heard anything. She was immediately on her guard against this intruder. A brief memory of the encounter at Berkeley with the two strange men flashed through her mind.

However, Kat's senses immediately relaxed when she saw it was Dave. He was fully undressed, and she knew his intentions.

Dave just smiled as he opened the glass door to the shower and stepped in. He pulled her warm, wet body towards him. The bathroom rapidly steamed up.

Dave dropped Kat off at the hospital and gave her his cellular phone. "Call Helen at this number when you need to reach me. She can reach me over the police radio. Otherwise, I will see you back here at four thirty. Okay?"

"Sure, that will be fine. I want to find Trapper and see how he's doing with fixing our cellular phone and replenishing our supplies." Kat slammed the door and blew him a kiss as she hurried down the walkway to the hospital entrance.

Dave watched Kat hurry down the sidewalk for a moment before pulling away from the curb. He smiled to himself and wondered what gossip Helen would spread around town when she found out about Kat.

Kat entered Don's room to find him sitting and impatiently

flipping TV channels with the remote control. "They sure don't have much in the way of TV up here, do they?" Don asked — more as a complaint than a question.

"How are you feeling?" Kat asked, surveying his bandaged leg.

"It hurts like hell, and I'm bored," Don replied.

"I know," Kat said. "But, you're going to have to put up with it a little longer."

"Yah, well the doc says the same thing." Don grimaced as he shifted positions.

"Don, you know I have to get back out there to complete my study, don't you?" Kat asked.

"Yah, I know. And I can't go with you," Don answered. "This was my big chance to help in an important study, and I blew it."

"You didn't blow anything," Kat argued. "In fact, you may be quite helpful to me being right here."

Don looked at Kat. "I don't understand. How can I be helpful to you here in this hospital bed?"

I'd like to leave the computer here with you, as you requested earlier. If we can get the cell phone fixed, then I can communicate with you here. You could still enter data and help us with the computer work, just as we planned."

"Who is going to take my place in the field? You can't go out there with just the two of you."

"Dave Parsons, who is the police officer here in Soldotna,

147

will be going with Trapper and me." Kat said. "He's the one who rescued us when you got injured."

Don thought this through, and said, "I think that is a good plan. Okay, I'll work with you from here. I can keep up with the daytime soap operas in between work — that is, if they have soaps up here." Don laughed for the first time since the bear attack.

Kat left Don to seek out Trapper and to call Dr. Ravens. She found a phone in the lobby of the hospital and dialed Victor Ravens' number.

"Hello, this is Dr. Ravens."

"Hi, Victor. It's Kat."

"Well, hello there. How's everything going?" Victor asked.

"We've had our share of trouble," Kat replied. She told Victor about the bear attack and Don's injuries. She was quick to explain that Don was okay and was recovering nicely in the hospital.

"Perhaps you should call off the expedition, Kat. It's not worth the risks. You're short-handed, and it's dangerous. You not only have to look out for shady characters but also wild animals." Victor argued.

"No. I don't want to quit now. Besides, I have a new recruit. He's a police officer here in Soldotna who's pretty knowledgeable of the region where we have to go."

"All right. I guess it may be okay. Having a police officer for this seemingly dangerous mission is probably a step up from having a green graduate student," Victor admitted. "However, you

148

still need to be wary. We don't know who those men are who attacked us, or who they represent. Now, you be careful."

"Okay, I will be careful. I have to go now. I've got a lot to do." Kat disconnected from Victor and immediately dialed another number.

When the voice at the other end of the line answered, Kat said, "Hello, this is Dr. Jones. How are you, sir?"

Kat listened intently to the man and addressed his questions. "Yes, sir. I know it's dangerous. But, the bear attack was an accident, which could not have been avoided. No, sir. We are continuing with the biological survey as soon as we get some equipment repaired. I have a police officer who will be replacing the injured student. And, Trapper is still on the expedition team. Yes, sir. I think Trapper is working out well. Thank you for locating him for me. He's quite familiar with the wilderness, and I trust his judgment. I know that time is critical here. But, I don't think we will lose much more time. We built in some weather contingencies; so we aren't too far off schedule. Yes, sir. I will try to call in two days, when we have made some progress in getting back to the interior."

Kat hung up the phone and looked at her watch. It was almost noon. She wondered how to get in contact with Trapper. She walked outside of the hospital. The bright sunshine caused her to squint but warmed her skin. It felt good to be in the fresh air again. Just as she was deciding where to go and whether she should call Helen on Dave's cellular phone, Dave drove up in his police cruiser

149

with Trapper in the passenger seat. "Are you hungry?" Dave asked.

"Sure, I'm glad you found Trapper. I was wondering how I was going to find him," Kat said as she climbed in the back seat. She felt funny sitting behind the cage enclosure that separated the front and back seats.

"Well, actually, he found me. I came out of the Riverside Inn where I was talking to Josh, and he was standing by the car."

Trapper nodded to Kat, and said, "I got the phone fixed. I also got a spare battery pack."

"That's good. We'll need the phone to be in communication with Don periodically. I'm leaving the computer with Don, because I want to give him scientific data over the phone. Besides, it might not hurt to have a contact back in civilization. I'd like to leave tomorrow. Can we be ready?"

Dave said, "I can be ready. I have already taken the time off."

Trapper grunted. "I can leave now."

I wonder if I am ready for this? Kat thought.

Chapter 15

The Hot Springs

Elice and Joslyn awoke to the smell of coffee and bacon frying on the fire. They crawled sleepily out of their tent to find Chad and Jasper sitting by a campfire, cooking and talking. Elice said as she approached the men, "I didn't know you brought bacon. I thought all we had was the freeze-dried food packets."

Chad stirred the bacon. "I knew how you enjoyed bacon and eggs cooked over the campfire. And, they won't keep. So, I thought it would be good to have real food for our breakfast early in our trek. This will be all until we finish the biological survey and get back to town."

The four of them sat around the fire, eating their breakfast and talking. Eventually, Chad said, "Okay, now we have to get to work. I want to start collecting samples from the river and its tributaries upstream of the village." Chad pulled out a map of the area, which showed the river winding through the valley and hills. He pointed out the prominent landmarks such as the Twin Lakes and Skilak Glacier. "Joslyn, I would like you and Jasper to go here, to these tributaries and measure the temperature, oxygen content and acidity of the water. Also measure the depth and width of the streams along the way. Elice and I will hike to these tributaries over here and begin collecting biological samples. We'll meet back here at camp at the end of the day. Whoever gets back first can start dinner. Any questions?"

"Just one," Joslyn said as she looked over the map. "I don't think I know where to access the streams in these places." Joslyn pointed to three places on the map.

Jasper looked briefly at the map, and said, "I know the way. It shouldn't be a problem."

While Jasper cleaned up after the breakfast, the other three

152

got the equipment sorted out for the two treks. Once the backpacks were ready, the camp was cleaned and secured.

Jasper led Joslyn off to the west. Elice and Chad headed to the north. Jasper and Joslyn walked quickly along an old path that led up the hills and over a ridge. Joslyn hummed along the way, thoroughly enjoying the tranquility of the area. An eagle screeched above them as they hiked. Jasper stopped only long enough to commune briefly with the eagle. They continued to hike along a narrow game path until they came to a small stream. Joslyn stopped to check her map. "This is the first stream we're suppose to sample," she told Jasper. "But, let's go to the next stream and sample that one first. We have to come back this way, anyway, and can get our samples here at the end of the day."

Jasper and Joslyn hiked for another hour before they came upon the second stream. They then turned north to follow the stream to its headwaters. The going was rugged; however, Jasper found the best route that was available. As they maneuvered through the shrubs and brush, Jasper pointed to a distinctive plant that had long woody stems, like single branches of small trees. Each stem was covered with a multitude of thorns, each about an inch long. At the end of each woody stem was club-like growth that, at this time of year, was a closed flower. "Don't touch this plant — it's called Devil's Club and its thorns are very dangerous. If you brush against the thorns, they'll break off and work their way into the skin, and they are very tough to get out."

Joslyn studied the thorns. She gingerly stepped over the plant and followed Jasper up the trail. "So, is this plant a weed up here in Alaska?"

"No," Jasper replied without turning around. "Its roots are very important to my people. We use it for certain medicinal purposes."

They walked in silence for another half hour. As Joslyn came around the bend, she saw Jasper squatting near the stream with his backpack on the ground. He looked up and said, "This is the place marked on the map. You want to sample here?"

Joslyn stopped and looked around the area. She put her backpack down and took out her map. "Yah, this is the place. Let's get out the equipment."

They donned their fisherman's waders and walked gingerly in the stream. They used the instruments to measure the temperature, oxygen content, and acidity of the water. The readings indicated that nothing unusual was coming downstream to alter the water chemistry. The slippery rocks in the stream caused them to walk slowly. Finally, they were finished and packed up to move on to the next site. As they were about to leave, they heard the long howl of a wolf in the distance. Joslyn froze at the sound and looked at Jasper. He shrugged, and said, "don't worry. He's a long way off."

Jasper and Joslyn hiked to the next site, and they made their collections. Joslyn was apprehensive the whole time and could not keep her mind off the wolf howl. They sampled the four sites they had been assigned. It took them the whole day. By the time they reached the camp, they were exhausted. As they walked into camp, they found some strangers awaiting their arrival.

Elice and Chad had hiked about two hours to reach their first site. When they got to the site, they took off their backpacks and flopped to the ground. They sat that way for a few minutes catching their breath. "Whew, that was a long, hard climb," Elice gasped.

"Yes, it was," Chad replied. "Now, we have to muster the energy to sample the organisms in the stream. Are you ready?"

"Yes, I guess I am. What is it you want me to do?" Elice asked.

"I'll have you follow me with the sieving screen and jars, while I sample with the net, here. The water is cold, so we should get going and finish as quickly as possible." Chad started getting the gear together.

He took the net and waded into the stream. He moved in an upstream direction from one spot to another. He placed the net downstream so that when he disturbed the rocks with his feet, the insect larvae, snails, and other organisms would drift with the water current into the awaiting net. Chad checked the net each time to see what he collected. Then he turned to Elice who was holding the sieving screen, where he inverted his net over the screen. Chad took the screen and ran water through it, washing the organisms and detritus, thus removing the loose sediment. He took one of the jars and washed the sample into the container. They managed to collect the samples in good time. Back on the bank, he poured some alcohol used for scientific research into the jar to preserve the organisms. He would take them back to the laboratory where the organisms would be identified and counted. Once he knew the number and kinds of species in each sample, he could tell whether the stream was healthy or not. From his crude observation as he was collecting, this stream looked pretty good. Then, they packed up and started hiking up the trail to the second site. This hike was equally rugged, but they kept hiking until they reached the second site. The difficult hiking was wearing them out. At this rate, it would take three or four days to sample all the sites.

The second stream site was not as good as the first. Chad could tell from all of the sediment covering the rocks in the stream that something out of the ordinary was going on in the upper reaches of the watershed. The sediment did not look like the result of bank failure and soil erosion that would come from lumbering activities. The sediment was largely composed of coarse sand and gravel, which indicated that some placer mining might be occurring in the stream. If this was true, it was consistent with what Sir Hilary and Senator Hodges suspected.

Elice interrupted his train of thought. "Chad, what are you looking at?"

"Oh, I guess I was thinking more than looking. I was wondering if this heavy sediment load is because of some recent placer mining in the area."

"Is placer mining is very destructive to the streams?"

"Yes. Generally, diversion channels are constructed from the main stem of the stream, and the water and substrate are run through these bypass ditches. Machinery consisting of hydraulic lifts and vibrating screens are used to sort the gold from the substrate. However, some operations are mobile and the machinery is put right in the stream. The substrate is sifted through floating "wash plants" and discarded in disarray in the stream afterwards. The destruction of the stream habitat and surrounding bank areas causes a tremendous amount of sediment being washed down the stream. So, environmental impact has been severe in the North Fork tributaries of the Kenai River.

"Can't the streams be restored?" Elice asked as she worked her way upstream to where Chad was standing?

"Much of the recent technology in placer mining has been designed to minimize environmental impact. However, the cost for repairing environmental damage from techniques that are not environmentally friendly can exceed any potential profit." Chad shifted his position to make room for Elice on the slippery stones in the stream. "I can't tell how far up the stream the sediment movement had originated. I think that checking out the source of the problem will have to wait another day. Right now, we have to collect more samples."

Chad and Elice were able to sample three sites before it was time to head back to camp. Chad said, "According to the map, we might be able to cut through this pass to get back to camp. Do you think we should take this route?" Chad pointed to the map.

Elice scrutinized the map. "I think that would work. It looks like it isn't going to be much harder than what we've just traveled. Chad, are all your collecting trips this difficult?"

Chad continued packing his pack. "Oh, I don't know. I didn't think this was bad. Besides, I'm glad I got the opportunity of being out in the beautiful wilderness of Alaska again with you."

Elice smiled. "Yes, it has been a long time, hasn't it? Even with the difficult trek, it's been fun. It's too bad we only get to see each other when business calls."

Chad thought about her statement. "Has your profession been rewarding to you? I mean, are you happy with your position at the university and staying here in Alaska?"

"I guess I never thought about it like that. I have been happy with my position. I don't have much to compare with the university, other than the life in the Native village where my relatives are living." Elice absently rubbed her bare leg as she talked. Chad followed the movement of her hands with his eyes and noted her nicely shaped leg. Elice continued. "I guess I'm not interested in leaving Alaska — certainly not right away. I'm making pretty good progress right here with my work. But, what about you?"

Before Chad could answer, they heard the howl of a wolf. It was hard to tell exactly whether the wolf was close or at a distance.

Both Chad and Elice stopped to listen. Soon they heard a second howl from a different direction. "Brother wolf has made a kill and is telling his mate," Elice said. They listened a few moments longer, but the only sounds were the rushing water of the stream and birds rustling in the brush.

Without a word, both Chad and Elice decided it was time to go. They hoisted their packs and began making their way to the pass Chad had noted on the map. After awhile, they came to the pass, which was little more than a long, narrow valley between two ridges. They hiked along this quiet valley for about two kilometers before they came to what appeared to be a dead end. In front of them the valley rose sharply into a ridgeline. They were at the end of a horseshoe valley. Chad checked the map, which did not show this feature. He was puzzled for a moment and checked his map again. He had not read the map wrong — the map was in error. He and Elice searched for a passage up and over the ridgeline. They found one slightly to the left and worked their way up the cobble and boulder-strewn hillside. They reached the ridge after a half hour of picking their way around boulders and loose cobble.

When they reached the top they stopped to rest. "Whew!" Elice exclaimed. "This doesn't get any easier, does it?"

Chad leaned against his pack and surveyed the area around them. Then he jerked upright and stared at a wisp of smoke coming from behind a boulder about twenty meters from where they were sitting. He motioned Elice to keep very still. Chad left his pack there and walked toward the smoke, careful not to make a sound. As he approached the boulder, he suddenly relaxed and stood upright. Then, he disappeared from Elice's view around the boulder. He soon reappeared. He smiled. "Come on. I want to show you something." He picked up his pack and led Elice to the smoke. As they came close to the boulder, they could smell the sulphur. Chad watched the realization come into Elice's eyes that the smoke was actually steam coming from hot springs hidden behind the boulder. The spring was a small, clear pool with the distinctive sulphur smell permeating the air. The pool was about three feet deep and roughly circular with a flat bottom, except for the narrow crevice where the water came through the rock. At one end, a spillway allowed the excess water to spill out into a small stream of water that ran down the hillside on the opposite side of where Chad and Elice had just climbed.

Elice laughed. "I had forgotten that this area is known to have a few hot springs from the volcanic activity in this area of Alaska. I bet this is a pretty interesting spot in the winter with the snow all around."

"It looks like a hot tub, doesn't it?" Chad asked as he stooped to feel the temperature of the water. "I wonder if it's too hot to sit in it?"

"It does look inviting," Elice said. "Do we have time to try it out?" She didn't wait for an answer as she bent over to untie her hiking boots. Chad followed. Elice had her clothes off first, hesitated only a moment, and then entered the water. She exhaled loudly. To

Chad, the view of her exquisite body seemed so natural here in the wilderness with the boulder outlined behind her. Her breasts were buoyant in the water, and the clear water magnified the view. This aroused Chad.

Chad finished undressing, and it was Elice's turn to watch. He then stood upright, and their eyes met. They both smiled. Elice said, "Come on in. The water's great."

Chad stepped into the water and quickly sat down next to Elice. As he fully immersed his body in the water he felt the exhilarating feeling of the hot temperature permeating throughout his body. Their backs were against the boulder, and they looked out across the valley ahead of them. "What a view." Chad said, as he looked out at the vast wilderness ahead of them. "This is really beautiful."

Elice waved her arms back and forth under the surface, slowly stirring the water and feeling the warmth. "You were about to tell me whether you are happy with your career choice when we heard the wolf."

"Oh, yes," Chad said. "I'd forgotten. Let's see. I guess I hadn't really thought about my career choice. I was actually selected for my career, and so didn't have a lot of choice."

"How so?" Elice asked.

"Well, I'm not unhappy with my career. In fact, I don't think I could have chosen a better one." Chad shifted in his seat and stretched his legs to feel the warmth of the water. "A senator chose me to enter a special research institution after my Ph.D. So, he supported my education with the idea I would work with him when I finished. I don't know exactly why I was chosen. I don't know how many others were interviewed and evaluated by the senator. I do know that my interest in ecology and martial arts background were important factors."

"How so?"

"Well," Chad began again, "the research projects that we get involved with have a high probability of becoming adversarial with someone or another. Martial arts have trained me in both physical and non-physical confrontations. I think the Senator knew more about me than I thought he did. I guess he's been satisfied with me -- I haven't been fired yet."

Elice looked into Chad's eyes. "The last time we saw each other, you didn't have a particular girlfriend. How about now?"

Chad studied Elice's face for a moment. "There was a woman I was seeing pretty regularly back home. However, she didn't like my constant traveling and now is seeing someone else."

They sat there quietly for what seemed to be a long time enjoying the heat of the water, the tranquil wilderness, and each other's company. Finally, Elice broke the silence. "I wonder if we can find one of these hot springs every day?"

Chad replied, "If we did, we wouldn't get anything done."

Elice laughed. "Yes, but I'm not sure we would feel guilty about it."

"Yah, I guess you're right. But–" Chad stopped and put one hand firmly on Elice's thigh as he pointed to something with the other.

They sat there like statues staring at a large wolf not more than eight meters away, sitting on a rock watching them. The wolf didn't come any closer.

While not taking her eyes off the wolf, Elice moved up against Chad and whispered, "I don't think we should make any sudden moves. I believe the sulphur smell of the pool is too pungent for him. I suspect he's already closer to the smell than he would like."

"I agree. And, my gun is in the backpack." Chad replied.

They sat there watching the wolf watch them. Soon, the fear turned to awe as they looked at this beautiful, wild creature allowing them to simply watch him. They were also acutely aware of their nearness to each other.

Suddenly, the wolf turned and left, as if it had just realized it was late for an appointment, and disappeared among the rocks.

Chad and Elice watched him go, but did not shift their positions. Instead, Elice turned more towards Chad and laid her head upon his shoulder and rested her free hand on his arm. They remained that way for a little while, neither one saying anything. Chad leaned more toward Elice and lifted her chin so he could gaze into her eyes. He then softly kissed her.

Then Elice stood up, and pulled Chad up to her. They stood

there in the middle of the pool, hugging and kissing. Elice's warm body pressed against his took Chad's breath away. He could feel her soft breasts and hardened nipples against his chest. He stroked her back as they stood in the pool, oblivious to all else around them.

After their lovemaking, they slowly got dressed. Before they donned their packs, Chad drew Elice to him and gave her a long kiss.

Elice looked at Chad. "You know our relationship will forever be changed, don't you?"

"Yes, I know." Chad said, thickly. He cleared his throat and continued. "Maybe that's okay. I think we have always been closer than either of us realized. It was inevitable."

"Perhaps you are right." Elice said. "But, I know I will never think of you the same way again."

Chad and Elice hiked quickly down the trail. They knew they probably had spent more time than they should have at the top of the ridge. However, they both felt refreshed, and they both glowed just a little.

"Well, do you think Joslyn and Jasper will have dinner going by now?" Elice asked to make conversation.

"I suspect so." Chad replied. "I know Jasper can cook. I just don't know about Joslyn and campfires." But, then again, Chad's mind was on something other than food.

Chapter 16

Mystery at Camp

Chad and Elice walked into a very quiet camp. No one was around. They called for Jasper and Joslyn, but received no answer. Chad had thought that Jasper and Joslyn would get back before them. Then he saw Joslyn's backpack lying on the ground next to her tent. Elice called that she found Jasper's backpack and three strange packs.

Chad came over to look at the packs. He didn't find anything that gave the identity of who might own the packs. He knew one person was a woman and the other two were men. He found a gun in one of the packs.

Elice checked her tent, and Chad checked his. He found a cellular phone lying slightly under his sleeping bag, partially hidden from view. He pulled it out of the tent and stood up to look at it.

Elice joined him. "Where did you get that?"

"It was in my tent. I don't know whose it is." Chad played with the buttons and a series of numbers flashed on the digital display. He pressed send and the phone started ringing.

"Hello."

"Hello. Who is this?" Chad asked.

"Who are you?"

"Now, look here." Chad was getting angry. "I found this phone in my camp, and two of my people are missing. I need some answers fast."

The voice hesitated. "All right. The phone belongs to Dr. Katlyn Jones of Berkeley. She was–".

"*Kat is here?*" Chad exclaimed. "What is she doing here?"

"I was trying to explain to you. But, perhaps you should tell me who you are."

"My name is Chad Gunnings."

"Dr. Chad Gunnings of the Phoenix Environmental Research

166

Institute?"

"Yes."

"I've read most of your papers. Dr. Jones speaks very highly of you."

"And who are you?" Chad asked.

"I'm Don Peters, one of Dr. Jones' graduate students. I came on her biological survey up here. I got mauled by a bear and I'm recovering in a hospital in Soldotna. I have the computer and I'm suppose to be entering some data as Kat and Trapper collect samples. Dave Parsons, a policeman here in Soldotna is with them." Somehow, Don managed to summarize the entire story in 30 seconds.

"Okay." Chad said. "Let's see if we can figure out what happened here. Kat and her crew must have found our camp, which answers why there are three strange packs here. But, something must have happened, because two of my crew members are missing. But their packs are here. I found the phone in my tent, which must have been placed there by Kat so I would find it." Chad paused for a moment. "When was the last time you talked to her?"

"Yesterday. Kat called to tell me where they were on the trail and to check on me. She said she was going to an old Indian village that was vacated many years ago. I looked up a map on the Internet, so I could follow their progress. It gives me something to do. It's really boring here."

"Well, our camp is at the village. So, she was able to meet up with us — or at least part of my crew. Did she know I was here?"

Chad asked.

"No, I don't think so. At least she didn't tell me. I thought we were the only biological crew up here. What do we do now?" Don asked.

"I think I'm going to take a look around. I'll get back to you." Chad said.

"Oh, before I forget, Trapper has extra batteries for the phone in his backpack. It's a ragged looking thing. He wouldn't use one of the new ones Dr. Jones offered him."

"Okay. Thanks. I'll call back tomorrow." Chad turned off the phone and looked at Elice.

Elice had heard at least Chad's side of the conversation and had surmised the essence of what happened. She could see the concern in his eyes and encircled his arm with her own.

Chad's eyes softened as he looked at Elice. "We should look around the perimeter of the camp. Whatever happened here is a mystery. All we know is that Jasper, Joslyn, Kat Jones, and two of her men were here and are now gone. Robbery was not a motive, because nothing seems to be missing. We'll have to be careful — we don't know what we're dealing with. Let's stay in sight of each other." Chad surveyed the camping area as he talked.

Chad began walking in a circular fashion around to the left and Elice to the right. They walked in ever-widening circles crossing each other's paths. Chad stopped at a spot where the grass was crushed down in places, and several boot marks in the ground were evident. He stooped down and surveyed the area, touching the marks to feel whether the soil was crumbly or hardened, which would give some indication of the length of time since the marks were left. When he was satisfied that he had gleaned all available information from the area, he resumed his perimeter walk. They had widened their circle to a radius of ten meters from the center of the camp. Elice was on the opposite side, about twenty five meters from Chad when he heard her shout.

"Chad, over here — quickly!" Elice bent down over something and disappeared from Chad's sight.

Chad sprinted directly to Elice's position. As Chad came upon Elice, he saw her leaning over something lying in the grass, partially hidden by the tall grass and a large boulder.

Elice was tending to a man lying on his back in the grass. His scruffy-looking beard and hair were matted with blood. The man's left shoulder also was bloody from a wound. "Who do you think he is, Chad?"

Chad looked him over, but didn't recognize him. "I don't know. I wonder if he's one of the men that came into camp and fought our people?"

"How do you know there was a fight?" Elice asked.

"There's evidence of a struggle over there." Chad pointed behind as he leaned over the man.

The man groaned and tried to open his eyes. Chad partially lifted the man's head, checking for any injury to his neck and back of the head as he did so. The man groaned again and opened his eyes, trying to focus on the man leaning over him.

"Who ... who are you?" the man asked.

"I'm Chad Gunnings. And, who are you?"

"Trapper," the man said.

"I heard about you, you were with Kat Jones. What happened to the others?"

"Naw. I got shot here in the shoulder and must have hit my head when I fell." The man groaned again as he tried to move his arm.

"What happened? Who were these men?" Chad asked, with a little more gentleness in his tone.

"I don't rightly ... know. I ... I was scouting out the area when I heard shouts ... from the camp. I rushed back to see a fight between Kat and the others ... with some strangers." Trapper was struggling with his words. "I could see Kat fighting two men, and Parsons fighting a rather large one. The old Indian had been knocked out, and ... the black girl was putting up a pretty good fight before she got knocked down. The man who knocked out the girl ... saw me running towards camp, and pulled out a gun and shot me. That's ... all I remember ..."

"Well, let's get you cleaned up and take care of your wounds. Then, you can tell us what brought Kat and you to this region. We may be able to figure out what has happened," Chad said as he and Elice helped Trapper to his feet. This biological survey had turned into a very dangerous situation, and Chad didn't know why.

Chapter 17

Trapper's Story

Trapper was propped up next to the campfire, sipping some
. hot tea. His head was bandaged and his left arm was in a sling. Chad
had cleaned his wounds as best he could. A bullet had creased his
shoulder, but it was only a flesh wound. As Trapper had thought, he

had fallen and hit his head on a rock, which knocked him unconscious. All of the blood and his unconscious state must have made the men think he was dead.

Chad and Elice were sitting near Trapper. Chad was the first to speak. "I found Kat's phone in my tent and talked to a guy named Don Peters. He told me a little about Kat's expedition. What I don't know is why you came to the Sqilantnu area, and who those men were and what they wanted. Maybe you better tell us what you know. Start with your leaving Soldotna."

Chad and Elice waited for Trapper to speak. Trapper collected his thoughts. He wasn't much of a story teller and preferred to listen more than talk. However, he knew this was important and that Kat might be in real trouble. Only the three of them could muster any kind of rescue attempt.

"Well, we left Soldotna a couple of days ago. There were three of us — Kat Jones, a man named Parsons, and me. We left Peters in the hospital to recover from a bear mauling."

"Yes, that's what Peters told me over the phone," Chad said. "Parsons is with the Soldotna police, right?"

"He's the only police in that town," Trapper corrected him.

"Why don't you continue," Chad said.

"The first day went okay on the trail. We didn't have any trouble along the way. I wasn't sure about Parsons, because I didn't know much about him. Peters was pretty much a maverick on the trail, and I was afraid that Parsons wouldn't be much better. But, I

173

could tell that he was pretty experienced in the backwoods. He and Kat talked most of the time. I think she was glad he was along. I'm not much of a talker. Kat had told me early on that we were coming to this place and gave me the maps so I could lead us here."

Trapper paused. Then he added, "We hiked well into the evening that first day, because we had good light, and those two didn't seem to be getting tired. When we had camp set up, Kat called Peters on the cell phone and talked to him some. She had him search some files on the Internet about this area the Indians call Sqilantnu. I didn't pay much attention to her when she was talking about it to Parsons. But, I heard her say that some sort of massacre happened here a long time ago to the Indians who used to live here. She told Parsons that she thought the mystery of this place had some connection to the strange feeling she had that someone didn't want her to do this survey."

"What did she mean by that?" Chad asked.

"All I know was that she had been attacked by a couple of men on the Berkeley campus before coming up here. She had told me that, because she wanted me to know that it might be a dangerous trip." Trapper paused to shift positions.

"I wonder if they were the same two men who attacked us at the airport in Anchorage?" Chad looked at Elice, but spoke to no one in particular.

Trapper continued. "The next day we started on the trail right after breakfast and arrived here in the afternoon. I remember that Kat was surprised to find this camp already set up. She wondered who it belonged to. We snooped around a little. Then, Kat found a knife in one of the tents that she recognized as belonging to you. She was pretty excited to think that you were here on the Kenai Peninsula."

"Kat gave me that knife after we graduated from school," Chad explained.

Trapper continued with his story. "She pulled out the phone to call Peters. Before she could make the call, two people walked into camp — an Indian and a black woman."

"Yes, they're my colleagues." Chad replied.

"They hadn't met before. But the black woman knew Kat, or at least knew her work. What were their names, again?" Trapper asked.

Elice said, "The woman is Joslyn, and the Dena'ina is Jasper."

Trapper studied Elice. "Well, anyway, they talked for awhile about their trips and what they were doing. Kat and Joslyn seemed excited that they were both there for the same reason. They were surprised that neither had known that the other was there — especially because of the close working relationship that you and Kat had." Trapper looked at Chad as he said that.

"Yes, I wonder why we didn't know the other was in the area." Chad was thoughtful. Then something occurred to him. He picked up Kat's cell phone and pushed a button that flashed through the numbers stored in the memory. There was the number he had used to call Peters. It was in the first memory bank. He scanned through other numbers. And, there it was — a number he recognized. He called it.

"Hilary here."

"Sir Hilary, this is Chad Gunnings." Chad paused to let it register.

"Chad, what a surprise. Senator Hodges is here. Let me put you on speaker phone." Chad heard a click.

"Dr. Gunnings, it's so good to hear from y'all. Where are you calling from?" The Senator asked.

"I'm calling from the Kenai, and I'm using Kat Jones' cell phone."

There was a pause. Senator Hodges was the one to answer. "So, you and Dr. Jones have met up with each other. That's good. Now, you can work together."

"Why didn't you tell me that Kat was also leading an expedition? And why didn't you tell her that I was out here?" Chad asked.

It was Sir Hilary who answered. "Dr. Jones' expedition was not part of PERI. Dr. Ravens had given me a call to ask for assistance. He told me about the attack on campus that they suspected was connected to her previous study up there on the Kenai. He said that Kat wanted to mount an expedition to check out the situation and see if the environmental conditions were getting worse. I talked to the senator, and we decided it would be a good idea to subsidize her expedition. Because we weren't sure of the connection of the attack with her study, or with the tense political climate there in Alaska at the moment, we decided we would keep the two expeditions separate. We didn't want your effort to be jeopardized if there was a problem specifically with Dr. Jones' study, and the people up there were watching her closely. On the other hand, we didn't want her to experience any more difficulty. We had seen her study plan and knew her biological survey would be conducted in a different part of the Kenai River watershed than yours. By combining the two surveys and letting both of you contact each other, we ran the risk of advertising a much larger scale expedition than each of you alone. We don't know Congressman Masserman's position, and we thought it prudent to keep this low key. After Kat's run-in with the grizzly, and having to retreat to Soldotna, she wanted to redirect her survey to the same area you were in. I didn't object, but neither did I offer her any information about your expedition. We knew there was a good chance that you two would run into each other. We didn't see a strong reason to inform either of you at the moment. We decided we would deal with it when the time came. I guess that's now. So, what have you and Kat decided to do?"

"Kat and I haven't discussed it, yet. She's been kidnapped — as well as Joslyn and Jasper."

"What?" both Sir Hilary and Senator Hodges responded simultaneously.

"Something dangerous is happening here, and I don't know

what it is. When Dr. Morningside and I returned to camp, we found it empty. We discovered an injured man named Trapper, who had been with Kat on her expedition. He explained a little of what had happened. Some men came into the camp, shot Trapper, and took the rest by force. Dave Parsons, a police officer who was with Kat, has also been kidnapped. So, there are the three of us here. In the morning, we're going to try to track them and find out where our colleagues have been taken.

"Listen to me, Chad," Sir Hilary said in the most serious tone Chad had ever heard him use. "We suspected this was a very serious situation up there, but we didn't know how serious. You have to be careful with whom you talk. Tell me, is Kat's graduate student still in the hospital?"

"Yes."

"Tell him to be careful, too. We don't know how much control Masserman has in that region. For all we know, he may have the police in his back pocket, as well. I warned Kat about taking Parsons with her, but she insisted that he couldn't be mixed up with Masserman or anyone else, for that matter. I hope this Parsons didn't lead her into something."

"I don't know Parsons. But, Trapper seems to think he's pretty good, and he was fighting the men alongside of Kat and the others. You may be right about contacting the state police, however. All it takes is one police officer to be on the take to make our lives difficult. What do you suggest?"

178

Senator Hodges said, "We are going to contact a special unit to send up there to help y'all. This unit can be trusted. In the meantime, y'all be careful and don't get yourselves in any deeper."

"How will this unit find us? We aren't going to stay here in camp. We're setting out tomorrow to find our friends," Chad said.

"We'll send the unit to the Sqilantnu where your camp is currently. Leave some sign of which direction you are going. They'll be able to find you. The unit's commander is Major Reed. Be careful!"

Chad then hung up and immediately called Don. He filled him in on finding Trapper and what had happened to the others. He also explained to Don that he shouldn't talk to anyone at the hospital, or to the police, about this situation. It wasn't clear who could be trusted. Until Chad found out more information, they would be operating on their own. Chad told Don that he would serve as their outside contact, and he would assist Chad whenever possible from where he was in the hospital.

Elice and Trapper had heard Chad as he conducted the two phone calls and generally knew what was going on. However, Chad filled them in on exactly what he had learned from talking to the two men at PERI.

As he was explaining the situation to them, he got an eerie sensation that made him turn to look out from the camp. He saw two men walking into camp with their hands raised. Chad jumped up, as did Elice, and he positioned himself away from her and Trapper as the men approached. Trapper struggled to rise to his feet, and stood there unsteadily, still weak. As the men got closer, Chad and Elice both recognized them as being the warriors who attacked them at the airport and who were with Masserman. Chad looked around for his pack to get his gun.

One of the warriors saw the anxiety on Chad's face and knew what he was looking for. He spoke up. "Do not fear. We do not mean any harm. We wish to talk."

Chad looked at first one, then the other. Both warriors were unarmed, except for knives. They both kept their hands raised. Chad stood back as the warriors approached. The warriors went directly to the campfire and sat down cross-legged. Chad squatted but did not sit.

The warrior who had spoken before, spoke again. "I am Keeva. He is Two Feathers."

"What do you want?" Chad asked. Both Elice and Trapper watched the warriors carefully.

"We come to help," Keeva said.

"Is this a trick?" Chad asked. "You attacked us at the airport. And, you work for Masserman. What makes you think we can trust you?"

"We have been sent by Masserman to help you."

"Masserman sent you to help? I don't trust Masserman. I think he's behind the kidnapping."

Keeva shook his head. "You are wrong. It was not

180

Masserman. He is a friend of the Dena'ina and is trying to protect their lands. He sent us to watch you and to help you if you needed the help. So, we are here."

"But, you attacked us when we arrived at the airport," Chad said. "That's not a sign of someone who wants to help."

"We did not mean for it to go that far," Keeva said and shrugged his shoulders. "We wanted to scare you off from your expedition. We underestimated your fighting abilities. We will not do that again."

"But, why did you want to scare us off?" Elice asked.

Keeva looked at her. "Masserman thought your presence would stir things up. He was still investigating what was going on back here in the mountains. He wasn't sure whether the Dena'ina would be further hurt if things got out of hand. He was close to finding out who was behind the Kenai Catastrophe that occurred many years ago. He also thought that the catastrophe was linked to the environmental problems that are occurring in the Kenai River today."

"Why didn't he tell us all of this when we met with him in his office?" Chad asked.

"He hadn't completed his investigation of you. He didn't know whether you could be trusted. The person behind this has many connections around Alaska. Masserman has had to conduct a secret investigation and couldn't trust many people."

"Is that why you got involved?" Chad asked.

"Yes. Masserman knew that we are the Warrior Society and that we help our brothers and sisters with difficult problems. We prefer to conduct our affairs peacefully. However, we are trained as a paramilitary group and can use force, if necessary. Masserman called us in to help with the investigation and to protect him, as well. Until he determined the extent of these illegal activities, he hasn't been too open to alliances, even with the Dena'ina, although those are the people he is trying to protect."

"So, Masserman took the position of preventing commercial logging, because he felt these companies were conducting illegal operations up here in the mountains?" Chad asked.

"Yes. He understands that the pressures of heavy logging in this area is affecting the environment. And, he felt that it was possible these companies were doing more than they should to damage the environment. However, he has discovered that it most likely is not the result of the commercial logging operations, but may be due to the logging company who is working under the guise of the Dena'ina."

"What do you mean, the Dena'ina? They aren't doing anything illegal, are they?" Elice asked.

"No, the Dena'ina are not doing anything illegal. But, Masserman thinks the white man who is heading the operation is doing some illegal mining in addition to the logging."

Elice asked, "What does this have to do with the catastrophe of a hundred years ago?"

"Johann Parker is the man who runs the logging company for the Dena'ina," Keeva said. "His grandfather before him began the company. Masserman thinks his grandfather actually started the mining and killed the natives from the village here to prevent discovery of his illegal operations. Johann and his father operated under the same secrecy. They use their logging, which is done at a low level and intended to be a financial resource for the Dena'ina as a front for the more lucrative, and environmentally damaging, mining business."

It all made sense. Chad had suspected a mining-imposed impact earlier when he was sampling the streams. Heavy mining will cause a tremendous amount of sediment load going down the tributaries into the Kenai River, thus affecting salmon spawning and survival. Without environmental controls to reduce the impact upon the river system, the pervasive mining could be devastating. And, because illegal mining activities were a serious matter in Alaska, keeping them a secret at all costs was indeed dangerous to anyone who interfered. So, Sir Hilary and Senator Hodges were right about the situation, but had the wrong man. If these two were telling the truth, then Congressman Masserman was an ally and not an enemy.

"Why are you here, now?" Chad asked.

"We saw what happened to your friends," Keeva said.

"You saw what happened? Then, why didn't you help then?" Chad asked.

"We were up on that ridge and too far away to help your

183

friends. We knew you were not among them, because we have been watching your camp. We followed the men who captured your friends. We know where they were taken, and can lead you to them." Keeva looked at Chad.

"Then, you will save us a lot of time because a rescue is exactly what we want to do. We will start tomorrow. We need a plan. What can you tell us about the place?" Chad asked.

They planned most of the night before getting some rest. The warriors retired for the night away from camp. Chad, Elice, and Trapper also relocated themselves away from the camp to guard against any unexpected intrusion.

As Chad lay in his sleeping bag on the grass next to Elice, he wondered how much he could trust Keeva and Two Feathers, and whether he had the right to endanger Elice and Trapper in something he regarded as his responsibility. He turned to look at Elice, who seemed so calm next to him. He then realized he had no right *not* to allow them to participate in this rescue attempt. It was a matter of honor, and friendship.

Chapter 18

Prisoners

Kat awakened and winced at the pain. Her neck was sore from the uncomfortable cot, and her side was sore from the fight last night. The fight. Now she remembered. They had arrived in Chad's camp yesterday afternoon. It took them awhile to discover that the camp was Chad's. She wondered why Sir Hilary had not told her that Chad was here on the Kenai. He must have had his reasons, but it seems that it would have made good sense for the two of them to have teamed up.

It wasn't long after they determined the owners of the camp that an Indian and a black woman walked into the camp and asked what they were doing there. Kat looked at the woman and asked her if she was Joslyn. Joslyn was startled at the woman's question. When Kat introduced herself, Joslyn was even more surprised. She was obviously familiar with Kat's work through Chad, but they had never met. The two women had begun comparing notes of their respective missions.

They talked about their biological surveys and the objectives of what they were trying to accomplish. Kat described the bear attack and explained how Dave Parsons came to join the team. Joslyn told about their being attacked by members of the Warrior Society at the airport. Hearing Joslyn's story, Kat told about being attacked by two men on the Berkeley campus, which led to her being here. The two were determined that their respective attacks were not by the same men. Kat further explained that she was being subsidized by Sir Hilary and PERI. This revelation astounded Joslyn. She had no idea that Kat's expedition and Chad's were sponsored by the same agency.

Kat remembered that Trapper left to scout around and to collect firewood. Dave and Jasper strolled over to the fire ring to talk separately. Kat remembered noting that Dave and Jasper seemed to know each other, or at least knew of each other. They were absorbed in conversation while Kat and Joslyn were trying to figure out the connections of their surveys. Finally, Kat and Joslyn tied together the pieces of the story as best as they could. They then joined Dave and Jasper by the fire ring.

Kat remembered looking up as three men walked into the camp. She stood abruptly as she recognized that two of the men were the same who had attacked her and Professor Ravens at Berkeley. As Kat stood, the others sensed that something was wrong and stood as well. They all separated a few paces from each other as the men approached.

The two larger men carried rifles casually resting in the crook of their arms and pointing to the ground. The smallest of the three men spoke first. "Well, hello again Dr. Jones. I thought we might run into each other again," Fred said as he smiled disarmingly, then looked at Dave. "Well, hello Parsons. Fancy meeting you here."

"What are you doing here, Fred?" Dave asked.

Kat glanced at Dave, questioning the familiarity between the two men.

"We just came by for a visit. We want to be neighborly," Fred said.

"Did you follow us? And, what do you want?" Kat asked.

Fred continued smiling. "What we want is for you not to be here. You should have listened to me when we met in California. This is none of your business."

"What is none of our business? We're here to conduct some biological surveys of the Kenai River watershed. What does that have to do with you?" Kat asked. She looked at Dave out of the corner of her eye. He was shifting his gaze from the men to the tents, where his gun had been left, and back to the men.

Fred looked at all four of the people who faced him. "I don't have time to explain to you. You are not wanted here, but since you are here — I can't let you go. You'll need to come with us to meet my boss."

"We have work to do here. We aren't going to intrude in whatever your business is. When we're finished, we'll leave — you can be assured of that," Kat said.

"Like I said, I can't let you do that. You will come with us." Fred said. Three of Fred's men sneaked behind Kat and the others.

"I don't think that's a good idea." Kat said as she tensed.

A thud distracted all of them. As Kat turned toward the sound, Jasper dropped to the ground unconscious. One of the men stood over him holding his rifle as a club.

In the split second that the attack on Jasper occurred, Kat jumped toward Fred, kicking him hard in the side, which knocked him into Bubb, causing them both to lose their balance. She continued moving forward to a third man standing by Bubb and who was swinging his rifle around at her. She went into a somersault underneath the swinging rifle and, from the ground, brought up her leg in a swift flip kick that caught him hard in the stomach, doubling him over. She then landed an axe kick to the man's back, which collapsed him to the ground. Kat was up and ready for the next move.

Dave got to Jasper's attacker before the man could raise his rifle to stop him. Dave punched hard in an uppercut, which snapped the man's head back and made him stumble backward. A second man moved forward and swung his rifle hard at Dave. Dave ducked and executed a punch to the man's ribs. The air went out of the man in a gasp. However, the man was able to catch his foot behind Dave's knee, which made Dave lose his balance.

While Dave was struggling with the second man, the third man leveled his rifle on Dave. Joslyn, seeing this, ran and jumped to push the third man. She hit him in the side causing him to shoot into the grass to the side of the fighting men. However, her light weight caused little more than a temporary shift in aim. The man swung a backhand, which connected Joslyn in the face, knocking her backwards over a log. She landed hard on the ground, knocking the wind out of her.

Bubb and Fred had regained their feet as Kat was fighting their comrade. Kat shifted her weight and threw a flying kick at Bubb. However, he was ready for her and moved slightly to the side. He grabbed her leg as it flew by, and flipped her to the ground. Without releasing his grip, he bent her leg until she thought it would break. Fred moved in and caught hold of her arms. Between the two of them, she was incapacitated.

Just then, Trapper emerged from the woods and shouted at the men. He held a machete high in the air and started running towards the camp. The man who had hit Joslyn quickly took aim and fired, hitting Trapper. Trapper hit the ground, dropping his machete. No more sound came from him.

With Dave on the ground, the man who had hit Jasper had recovered from Dave's punch and stuck the barrel of his rifle hard into Dave's neck. "You better quit right there." The man said between clenched teeth. Dave stopped moving.

Fred rose from where he had pinned Kat, breathing hard. "Okay, all of you get up, and don't cause anymore trouble. I don't want to have to shoot all of you. One of you guys go check on that man you shot."

The man who had shot Trapper went to check on him. He found him lying on the ground behind a boulder. He nudged Trapper with his boot, while he trained his rifle to Trapper's head. Trapper didn't move. The man could see blood coming from Trapper's head. "He's dead!" The man shouted.

Kat gasped and thought to herself. "Trapper dead?" She rose slowly, being controlled by Bubb, who now had one of her arms held tightly behind her.

Dave also rose slowly, with a gun barrel held solidly against his neck.

One of the men went over to help Joslyn to her feet. She was wobbly, and her face still stung. It was starting to swell a little.

190

Jasper was still unconscious.

Fred was now again in control. "Tie their hands -- we will take them with us. I think that Mr. Parker will want to talk to them. Get that Indian up, and let's get going."

Kat remembered they had hiked quite a distance until they came to a fenced in compound where they were now. It was a difficult hike — their hands were tied, and they were all injured. Jasper was particularly having trouble, still groggy from the hit on his head. However, he made no sound the whole way.

Kat turned to look at Joslyn, who was lying next to her in the small dingy room. Joslyn was just awakening. Joslyn groaned. Her face was bruised and swollen. "Where are we?" she asked. "Oh, yes. I remember. What are we going to do, Kat?"

"I don't know. I think Mr. Parker is not certain that he really wants to kill us. I think he's more troubled that his men brought us here instead of just killing us in the camp." This was not encouraging news to Joslyn.

Kat thought back to last night when they were brought to Johann Parker. She remembered her awful feeling when they walked through the compound gates. Many men were around the area, and most had guns. She wondered what they had gotten themselves into as they had been taken to the log cabin in the middle of the compound. A short and squatty Eskimo woman had met them at the door.

"Who are these people, and why did you bring them here?" The Eskimo woman demanded of Fred.

"Now, Miss Elsie, we brought these folks to see Mr. Parker. Don't make this any more difficult than it is now."

"What if he don't want to see them?" Miss Elsie glowered.

"You just ask him. Tell him that Dr. Jones is here," Fred demanded.

Miss Elsie muttered to herself as she turned and went back inside.

It wasn't long before Johann Parker appeared at the door. "So, we have the famous Dr. Katlyn Jones at my front door." Parker looked her over. Then he switched his gaze to Dave. "And, you must be the police officer, Dave Parsons. I'm so sorry you all had to come here." Parker scrutinized each one in turn. Then he looked at Fred. "Fred, take them into the cave to the holding room. I will join you in a minute." Parker abruptly turned and walked back into the cabin.

Fred and the other men took them to the back of the cabin, and they walked toward the cliff face. It wasn't until they were almost at the rock when Kat noticed there was an opening into the mountain. She marveled at how well it was hidden from view. Fred led them down the well-lit passageway and into a large room. Pine furniture lined the walls. A large knotty pine table was in the middle. Paintings of wilderness scenes were scattered among the rock walls. The furniture was comfortable as they waited for Parker.

Kat remembered wondering about the comfort of the

furnishings and what the room was used for. In fact, she wondered about the cave and the compound. Perhaps some answers would be forthcoming from Parker.

They didn't have long to wait. Parker came into the room, and without looking at the captives, started pacing alongside the table. Finally, he came to where Kat was sitting. "Why did you come back here to the Kenai?"

"I came back to continue my biological research on what is causing the decline in the salmon population here," Kat said.

"What have you found out?" Parker asked.

"We know that heavy sedimentation is causing a problem and curtailing the spawning of the salmon, particularly the King salmon. We also know that there are no known activities in this area to cause the extent of the sediment erosion. So, something illegal must be going on up here. I suspect that you have something to do with this. Am I right? You wouldn't have tried to scare us off and capture us if you didn't have a very good reason to stop us."

"You're very smart," Parker said. "However, I have too much invested in this operation to let someone like you bring it all down."

Kat pressed Parker. "And, what is your operation? It's more than logging, isn't it? From the machinery in the compound, it must be mining. Right?"

Parker turned and walked to a painting on the wall. It was a scene of an Indian village in very rocky terrain. The scene showed several Indians performing activities typical of a remote and ancient tribe. Some were tanning hides, while others were cooking over fires. Some warriors were walking into the village carrying game. "What do you know about what people call the Kenai Catastrophe?" Parker asked.

Joslyn recited what Jasper had told her. "The Kenai Catastrophe occurred many years ago at the camp where we were attacked by your men. It was an old village where the inhabitants were wiped out by some murderous band of renegades. No one knows who did it."

"That's almost right." Parker replied. "I know what happened."

Joslyn said. "Why didn't you report it to the authorities, if you knew?"

Parker laughed. "And tarnish the name of my own grandfather?"

"Your grandfather? But, why did he murder all those Dena'ina?" Joslyn asked.

"He only killed a few — the sick and elderly. He did this to drive off the rest. He did it to protect the operation — the same one I'm running now." Parker turned to face the captives. "And, now I am facing the same situation as my grandfather."

"My grandfather was one of those he killed." It was the first time Jasper had spoken.

Parker walked over to stare at Jasper. "Your grandfather was

194

in that village? Well, now, doesn't that beat all. Our grandfathers met all those years ago. Now, I get to kill you."

Dave glanced at Parker and started to stand up. A guard pushed him hard back into his chair.

"Parsons, I almost forgot you were here." Parker smirked. "I guess it's frowned upon to off a cop, isn't it?" Without waiting for an answer, Parker swiveled quickly on his heel to face Kat. "Where is Dr. Gunnings?"

Kat and Joslyn looked at each other. Kat responded. "I honestly don't know."

"Why isn't he here?" Parker demanded as he turned to Fred standing by the door.

Fred felt uncomfortable with this new attention from his boss. "I don't rightly know. I guess I thought he was with the others when we went into camp."

"*You idiot!*" Parker screamed. "He must be out there somewhere. Now, our plans will have to change."

"What can Gunnings do? He's only one man." Fred pleaded.

Parker glowered. "He's very cunning. Besides, we can't let him get back to town to get help. Dr. Morningside is most likely with him. And, she knows her way out of the Sqilantnu. We will have to go find them."

Parker headed for the door. "Lock them up in the holding cells in the back of the cavern. Then come to the cabin. And make it snappy." Parker left the room without a backward glance.

Kat heard her name being called. "Kat, are you there? Are you alright?" Kat recognized Dave's voice. She got up from her cot and walked to the wall separating their cells.

"I'm here. Is Jasper with you?" Kat asked.

"Yes, we're both in here. Jasper is still sore from the crack on his head. I think the lump on his head is still growing. Is Joslyn with you?" Dave whispered.

"Yes, and she looks pretty bruised too," Kat said as she looked at Joslyn. "What can you see from there?"

"All I can see is the passageway out of the small window in the door. A light down the passageway is what's allowing us to see a little," Dave said.

"We have to figure how to get out of here," Kat said. "I don't think that Parker is going to let us leave here. We also have to warn Chad. I know that Parker is going to send some men out to find him." Kat's voice had a sense of urgency in it.

Dave said, "I know. I've been thinking of how we can escape. I have an idea. When the guards come to feed us, we'll have to be ready. They'll be expecting something, so we'll have to be quick.. The guards are different from the ones who attacked us at camp. When the men open the door to your cell, they'll be watching you and Joslyn. Jasper and I will cause a distraction over here — maybe make like we are having a vicious fight. That distraction will probably only last a fraction of a second, so you'll have to be quick."

Kat thought for a moment. "Okay, I guess that's the best idea we have. Hopefully, they'll come to my cell first." Kat grinned at the thought of these 'gentlemen' coming to see her.

"Shhh," Dave whispered. "I hear someone coming. I think it's time."

Chapter 19

The Compound

The five hiked along the narrow ridge and climbed to a higher elevation. Above, an eagle circled looking for food. The flash of silver that came from the woman's black hair caught its eye. However, this was not food, and the hikers were disturbing any potential food source. So, the eagle let the air currents carry it off to the south.

The hikers toiled up the mountain, grim-faced, and quiet. They knew what they had to do, but only had the semblance of a plan. Much would be determined on the spur of the moment. Their tactic would be diversion and surprise. Chad had his .44 Magnum. Keeva and Two Feathers carried compound bows. Elice carried Dave Parson's pistol, found in his backpack at camp. All had knives, and Trapper had a machete. They carried lightweight mountaineer's cord, and Chad and Trapper had binoculars around their necks.

Chad had called Don the night before to enlist his assistance. Upon instructions from Chad, Don had searched available satellite imagery files on the World Wide Web to find shots of the Parker Compound. Using the map he had downloaded previously to follow Kat's progress and a description of the approximate location of the compound from Keeva, Don had worked all night on figuring out the coordinates to pinpoint the compound. Recent advances in the Geographical Information System (GIS) linked with satellite imagery to conduct landscape analysis made it possible for a resourceful computer specialist like Don to search remote areas of the Kenai Peninsula. The University of Alaska had been establishing a comprehensive database of satellite imagery of the state for research on permafrost and vegetation coverage. Don had been successful in tapping into the university files, and with the World Wide Web, locate aerial pictures, which he magnified to search land form features of the area.

Don found the compound on the mountain that matched Keeva's description. Two sheer rock faces of the mountain were apparent from Don's view on the screen. The rock face to the south backed up to the compound itself. A high chain-link fence enclosed a large area in front of the rock face that constituted the compound. Either end of the fence disappeared into the mountain to form a secure fortress. The gate in the center of the fence was the only entrance, and that was heavily guarded. Access from above was nearly impossible unless one could climb up the side of the mountain on the west side unseen from the compound.

The second rock face was on the north side and prevented any access from below. The northern rock face was natural, whereas the southernmost one was man-made, having been chiseled from the mountain to build the compound. Don scanned the electronic files showing the northern rock face, looking for any evidence of an entrance of some type. He located a narrow ledge and small opening in the rock that indicated some sort of air passage, he thought. However, the only way to get to the ledge was from above. And he couldn't be certain it would lead to the inner cave that Keeva said was there.

Don then searched the real estate files for property owned by Johann Parker. He found none. However, he found construction plans listed under the name Frederic Parker for the compound that were dated twenty years ago. Don figured that Frederic most likely was the father of Johann. The plans showed the location of the log cabin, guardhouse, and a couple of outlying buildings. Because of the age of the plans, Don couldn't be sure of the accuracy, but had passed all of this information to Chad in the morning. Don had noted that in the legend box of the plans was the name Judge. This was curious to him. So, he searched the files further for anything that might be linked to Judge. He found two sets of plans, simply called Plan A and Plan B. Plan A was older by two years and showed a hall and large room connected to the hallway. The only thing on the plan was dimensions of the hallway and room. No reference to materials, doorways, or windows were given. Don surmised that these were in fact plans for a passageway and cavern into the mountain. Plan B looked like an extension of the first and showed a longer passageway and two more rooms. Don couldn't tell whether the opening he saw at the northern rock face would connect to a passageway or not. However, the dimensions were about right to extend through the mountain from the south to the north.

Don had worked feverishly all night to come up with all of this information and had talked to Chad about five o'clock a.m. to relate all that he had uncovered. With a map, Chad plotted the location of the compound and studied the topography. He outlined the compound and mountain on a piece of paper. Together with Keeva and Two Feathers, who both had Special Forces training, they made a plan.

Now, they were toiling through the wilderness, avoiding the

roads and main paths, hoping to remain unseen. The sky was becoming overcast, which was helping to diminish the light and reduce the visibility. They came up to the mountain from the west, and stopped to rest and go over the plans once more. Trapper left them and began moving around the foot of the mountain to the south. The other four began their long, arduous climb up the steep incline.

Trapper reached his destination first. He came upon the road leading up to the entrance of the compound. He walked along the side of the road, keeping out of view from anyone observing the road. He stopped about two hundred meters from the compound. There was a bend in the road here, which hid him from view of the compound. He climbed up a small knoll to watch the compound. He could see the fence and guardhouse and men walking around. He watched for a half hour to detect a routine in the movement. With his binoculars, he scanned the compound, then moved his gaze up the rock face to the top of the mountain. He searched the shrubs and rocks along the top and side. When he was satisfied that he could see no movement on the mountain, he slid down from the knoll and disappeared into the brush.

The four worked their way up the mountain. When they were three quarters of the way up, Two Feathers split off and went to the south, following a track parallel to Trapper's. Chad, Elice, and Keeva continued up the mountain until they reached the top. They hiked to the edge of the rock face on the south, crept to the edge, and peered over and into the compound. They studied the activity below for a short time. Then they backed away from the edge and stood up. Chad looked through his binoculars at the road leading to the compound. He searched for Trapper, who came out from the trees, carrying brush that he had cut with his machete. It didn't take long for Trapper and Chad to locate each other. Chad signaled Trapper as they had agreed upon. Trapper then knew about how much time he had before the others would reach their positions.

Chad and Elice went to the north. Keeva went down the other side of the mountain to position himself at the fence line opposite Two Feathers. Chad and Elice came to the northern rock face and looked over the precipitous cliff to see if they could find the ledge that Don had located from the satellite imagery files. They could not see the ledge, so Chad stepped off measurements along the top of the cliff. Then, he marked where he thought the ledge might be located, based on Don's description. Chad tied off two lengths of mountaineer's cord to two trees near the place where he and Elice would descend.

When they were ready, Chad turned to Elice. "I wish I knew for sure how this was going to turn out. All I know is this is going to be dangerous. I know that my suggesting you stay here is out of the question. However, I would do anything not to put you in further danger. I already have two friends in there somewhere and must do what I can to find and help them."

Elice put her arms around Chad. "I would have it no other way. Besides, I can't help but think that whatever is going on today is linked to the past. There is a history of suspicious disappearances in this regions, beginning with the Kenai Catastrophe that occurred all those years ago. So, I will be in danger regardless, as I continue my studies of the Sqilantnu. And, don't forget I have friends in there, too. Also... I can't... think of anyone I would rather be with in this situation."

Chad kissed Elice.

"I'll rappel down first on my cord to see if we are in the right place," Chad said as he tied his cord on a belay clip. "You watch from here, and I'll signal you. I may have to come back up if we're in the wrong place. Remember that we don't even know if this is an entrance or not. We might find a false opening, and then we will have to go to our alternative plan."

With that, Chad dropped over the side of the precipice. He rappelled slowly, looking around as he went. When he reached the distance that Don had calculated for the ledge, nothing was there. Chad stretched out from the rock face as far as he could go and strained his neck to look to the right and left. On the right about ten meters away was the ledge. He called up to Elice, who was watching him. "I found it, but we are a little off -- about ten meters, I'd say. I'm going down a few more feet, then try to swing over to it. Do you see another tree closer to the point above the ledge?"

Elice disappeared from view, then returned a few moments later. "No, we're as close as we're going to get."

"Okay, watch me, so you can see the distance we're talking

about. You'll have to do the same thing I'm going to do." Chad lowered himself another two meters, and then started walking along the rock face to the left as far as he could go without slipping. He pushed off from the rock face and swung to the right. As he came against the rock face, he started running until the momentum stopped him short of the ledge. As his weight carried him to the rock face, he pushed off again and swung to the left, back to where he had begun. This motion carried him farther to the left, which would give him more momentum to hopefully carry him to the ledge. He pushed off as hard as he could and repeated the exercise, swinging again to the right. He made contact with the rock face about three meters to the left of the ledge. He worked his feet and legs to continue the swinging motion in the direction of the ledge. This brought him within reach of the ledge. He grabbed and clawed the rock ledge to keep from swinging away. He managed to hold on and clamber onto the ledge. He sat there regaining his breath. Then he stood up and leaned out to see Elice. He could just see her head sticking out from the top of the cliff, straining to see him. "It's not difficult at all," he lied. "You shouldn't have any trouble. Just lower yourself to where I tell you to stop. Then, I'll guide you as you swing to the left and the right as I did. Start when you're ready."

Elice prepared herself for rappelling. She had done this before, but it wasn't one of her favorite things to do. The toughest thing for her to do was to lean out over the cliff and begin the drop. It was like dropping off the face of the earth. It made no sense at all.

However, she leaned out over the cliff, her legs beginning to shake, then lowered herself down the rock face. Chad talked to her as she came down the cliff. He stopped her when she had gotten a little below where he was. "Okay, now start walking along the rock toward me," he said.

Elice did as he instructed. When she could go no farther, she pushed off from the rock face. However, it was a weak effort and it brought her back to where she started. Chad gave her encouragement. "That's the idea. Now, push off harder and keep your legs spread and braced against the impact when you make contact with the rock face. When you touch the rock, begin walking as hard as you can in the direction of the swing."

Elice began again. This time, she got a better push off the rock. As she approached Chad on the swing to the right, he gave her continued encouragement. As she approached the ledge the second time, it was apparent she wasn't going to make it. Chad couldn't reach her. Chad shouted to keep going and to go immediately into another cycle. If she let up now, she would lose her momentum. She did what he said, and on the third try, Chad was able to catch her hand and pull her to the ledge.

Elice didn't realize how exhausted she was from the exertion and stress. She collapsed on the ledge. As she was catching her breath, Chad tied off the ropes. He suspected they would need them again.

After a few moments, Chad said, "If you've recovered, let's

see where this passage leads." He pulled a Maglite from his pocket and turned it on. Its powerful little beam of light showed a narrow passageway that would require them to go sideways for an unknown distance. The height was barely enough for Chad's tall frame. In places he had to duck and squeeze through. The combination of low ceiling and narrow width certainly made the passageway claustrophobic. However, neither Chad nor Elice complained. At one spot, they had to crawl for about twenty meters. Chad, who was leading, could see some light coming from the distance. He looked at his watch to see how much time had elapsed since signaling Trapper. Finally, the passage came to an end. Through an opening barely able to accommodate his body he could see a larger passageway. Chad thought that this must be one of the passageways that Don had found in the plans.

Keeva had managed to get to his position on the opposite side of the mountain from Two Feathers without incident. He scouted around to see what the topography was like. He crept up to the edge to look over at the compound. He was pretty close to the top of the fence and could see the inner area of the compound clearly. He looked over to the other side of the mountain to see if he could spot Two Feathers. He couldn't see him, but knew he was hidden there and was ready to go in when the time came. Keeva looked over to the road for Trapper. Because of the bend in the access road, Trapper was out of sight, which was good. If Keeva could see Trapper, then others in the compound might also see him.

Keeva looked at his watch. The plan they had worked out had many alternatives because they were neither sure of the best way for accessing the compound, nor escaping. They suspected the compound was where Chad and Elice's colleagues might be hidden. The first uncertainty was whether the passageway that Chad and Elice were following would actually lead into the cave. They had two hours to determine whether this was a route of access. If not, they had to get back to notify Trapper. Otherwise, Trapper would start a fire with the brush he was collecting. This would possibly be a successful diversion to draw many of the men from the compound and distract the others so Keeva and Two Feathers could swing in on their ropes to scale the fence and drop inside the compound. Then the two Indians would disappear among the buildings and shrubs to be in position to take out any men trying to enter the cave where they suspected the hostages were being held. If the fire did not occur at the designated time, that would tell Keeva and Two Feathers that Chad had signaled Trapper, and they would move into Plan B. Plan B was more dangerous, because it meant that Chad and Elice would join Keeva and Two Feathers and go over the fence with them. Then they would have to make it to the cave undetected. This would be nearly impossible, unless the fire diversion was more effective than anticipated.

Keeva and Two Feathers saw the smoke from the fire simultaneously. The two-hour wait had ended. Perhaps this meant that Chad and Elice had found passage and not a plan gone wrong.

The two warriors watched the compound and waited. Soon, the alarm was sounded in the compound and men scurried around. The gate opened and two trucks holding about ten men drove out and up the access road to the fire. The gate closed part way after them. The two men in the guardhouse watched the fire and the trucks moving toward the fire. Other men were running to and fro in the back part of the compound. No one saw the two warriors swing out over the fence and drop inside the compound. The warriors quickly vanished in the underbrush near the rock face, one on either side of the compound. Hopefully, the mountaineer's cords would not be seen hanging against the rock face. They were brown like the rock, so there was a good chance of not being seen. The more colorful ropes had been sent with Chad and Elice, because they would have stood out against the rock face surrounding the compound.

Two Feathers sneaked to the guardhouse, because he was closest. The two guards were oblivious as they watched the fire. Two Feathers entered the guardhouse with his knife pulled. The guards heard the movement and turned, but not soon enough to cry out. Two Feathers dispatched both men quickly and efficiently. Now, the men at the fire would not be able to re-enter the compound unless others came to open the gate. Two Feathers returned to his position near the rock face.

Trapper emerged from the ravine leading up to the fence. He had been hiding there, waiting for things to happen. After starting the fire and adding fuel of live brush to cause much smoke, he had sneaked off into the woods and followed the ravine to the fence. He watched and waited. He saw Two Feathers enter the guardhouse and take care of the two guards. As Two Feathers returned to his position, he sneaked through the partially opened gate and into the guardhouse. He kept low below the window and reached to the console and pushed the button to close the gate completely. He heard the intercom calling. "Hey, Butch! What's going on out there?"

Trapper hesitated, then reached to grab the two-way radio. In a muffled voice he answered, "All's Okay. We're just waitin' for the others. Looks like they're gettin' the fire under control."

No answer. After what seemed like an eternity, a voice response. "Okay Jim. I didn't know you were in the guardhouse with Butch."

Trapper sighed. The man must have mistaken him for someone else. Anyway, this man had bought Trapper's story. Trapper crouched down to wait and watch. He looked at the men laying on the floor beside him. Then, he reached down to pick out the handguns from the holsters on the men's belts. He certainly knew how to use guns, having done plenty of hunting. However, he wasn't sure he wanted to use them on another human. He would have to wait to see what happened.

Keeva signaled Two Feathers. It was time.

Chapter 20

The Rescue

Keeva kept to the shadows of the rock face as he made his way around the perimeter of the compound. He jumped behind a truck to avoid two men walking briskly by. As they passed the truck on one side, he sneaked along the other side in the opposite direction. When Keeva rounded the front of the truck, he surprised a man sitting on a crate in front of the truck, whittling on a piece of wood. Keeva had not known he was there, but reacted instantly.

The man glanced up as Keeva rounded the truck. "What the ..." the man swung his knife in the direction of the stranger who suddenly appeared.

Keeva deflected the knife with his forearm, and swung his other hand in a karate chop that collapsed the man's windpipe. The man fell into Keeva's arms. Keeva dragged the man quickly behind the truck and hid him behind some brush against the rock face.

Keeva returned to the front of the truck and scanned the compound. He stared across the compound, trying to locate Two Feathers. Finally he saw him as he darted from one bush to another. Both Keeva and Two Feathers continued moving to the entrance of the cave until they were approximately twenty meters from the entrance. There was no cover from their positions to the entrance. Two Feathers saw Keeva behind the last piece of cover before the open space to the entrance. Two men were standing on either side of the cave entrance. The men stood slightly facing each other so that the one on the opposite side of the cave faced Keeva. The other man on Keeva's side was facing Two Feathers. Their positions were such that they had a good view of the entire compound. However, they were both focused on the distant fire, and did not see Keeva and Two Feathers creeping along the rock face.

Keeva signed to Two Feathers with hand signals: When I give a low whistle of the marmot, shoot the man on my side, the one facing you. Keeva scanned the compound to be sure no one was coming or observing the cave entrance. He took out an arrow and notched it in his compound bow. He glanced up to see that Two Feathers had done the same. Both Indians raised their bows at the same time and aimed at the men. Keeva gave a low whistle and let his arrow fly. A second later, Two Feathers' arrow flew to his target. Both men were hit in the chest and fell backwards into the cave.

Keeva and Two Feathers immediately sprinted to the entrance and grasped the men under the arms and dragged them further into the cave. They found a room near the entrance where they dragged the men. They quickly snapped off the arrow shafts and removed the men's shirts. They put on the shirts and donned the ball caps, tucking their long hair under the caps. They removed the pistols from the dead men and put them into their own belts. Keeva and Two Feathers then returned to the entrance, laid their bows on the ground flat against the wall, and stood guard at the entrance.

Kat stood against the wall behind the door. She saw the shadow of a face pass before the narrow window in the solid oak door.

Joslyn stood in the middle of the room where she could be seen. Joslyn saw eyes through the window gazing at her. The eyes pulled back as the door opened slowly.

Kat readied herself as the door opened. She stepped from behind the door and began to execute a high flip kick to the face, estimating the height of the man from an instantaneous glimpse of the figure coming through the door. When she was in the initial phase of her forceful kick intended to smash the nose of the man, she heard Joslyn exclaim, "*Chad!*" In the split second of executing her kick, she snapped her lower leg backwards to fold at the knee and aborted her kick just in time.

In that same moment, Chad saw the blur and ducked, rolling quickly under Kat's leg, and jumped to his feet in a 'ready' position. However, both Kat and Chad recognized each other instantly, and noticeably relaxed their stances. They hugged.

"Kat, I had no idea ..." Chad began.

"I know. Me either ..." Kat replied.

Their greetings only lasted a few seconds, and reality set in. Chad looked quickly around the room, taking in the surroundings. "I guess we should talk about this later. Right now, we have to get out of here. Kat, this is Elice." Chad motioned to Elice as she stepped into the room. "She's an anthropologist with the University of Alaska."

Elice and Kat exchanged quick greetings and appraising looks that transferred much information in a second; Elice gave Joslyn a hug.

A desperate voice sounded through the wall. "*Kat, what's going on? Are you two all right?*"

"Yes, Dave. We're okay." Kat replied. "Chad is here. We're okay." She repeated.

Kat looked at Chad. "How did you get in here?"

"It wasn't easy," Chad answered as he moved toward the door. "First, we hiked up a big mountain, then scaled down a steep cliff, then squeezed through a narrow passageway. We overcame a guard walking down the hall towards your room. He happened to have a large key, which fit your door. Hopefully, it will also fit the door of the next room, too. Wait here — we don't want too many people in the hallway."

Chad checked the hallway. It was clear, so he slipped next door and tried the key. It opened. "Hi, I'm Chad," he said to Dave. Then he noticed Jasper's bandaged head. "Hi, Jasper. You okay?"

"I'm fine." Jasper replied. "Just a headache." He said, as an afterthought.

"We're going to get you outta here. Come on." Chad led the two men back to the other room.

When they returned, Kat surprised Chad with another hug. "Elice told me that Trapper is still alive," she exclaimed. "I thought they killed him."

"No, he's not dead. In fact, he's providing the distraction for us at the moment," Chad said. "But, it won't last for long. Now, we gotta get going. Elice, take them back the way we came. I'm going to find Keeva and Two Feathers."

"Who are they?" Dave asked.

"They're of the Warrior Society. They've come to help us," Chad replied.

Jasper looked at Chad. "Our brothers are truly brothers. That is good." Jasper and Chad gave each other a knowing glance. Dave and Kat looked at them in bewilderment.

"Go now. I'll catch up with you," Chad ordered.

"Be careful. Kat said Parker and his men will be coming soon to get them," Elice pleaded. Kat caught the look that Elice gave Chad and smiled.

Elice led Kat, Dave, Joslyn, and Jasper deeper into the cave. They were part way past a room when the door opened. An old man stood there with his mouth open. It took a moment for it to register with him what was going on. Before he could say anything, Dave clapped his hand over the mouth of the old man and pulled him backwards into the room. The others followed.

"Quiet, old man," Dave hissed. "I don't want to hurt you. I'm going to remove my hand. If you shout, I'll knock you out. Understand?"

The old man nodded.

"Who are you?" Dave asked as he removed his hand.

"*Who are you?*" the old man demanded. "I know who I am."

"We're *visitors*, trying to find our way out," Joslyn answered the man as she approached him.

The old man peered closely at her, then at the others. "You must be those environmentalists who're trying to destroy our business. Johann told me about you. What are you doing here? You shouldn't be here."

216

"We know. We don't want to be here. That's why we are leaving," Joslyn said.

Kat and Jasper watched the hallway. Dave released his hold on the old man and searched the room for another exit. None could be found.

"Well, get on with it. And, leave me alone. I have work to do," The old man turned his back to them, believing the meeting was over.

Dave clasped the old man's arm lightly. "I'm sorry, old man. But we're going to have to tie you up, until we can get away."

"You'll do no such thing." The old man glared at Dave.

Dave maneuvered the old man to a chair and tied his arms and legs to the chair. He stopped the old man's protesting by putting a piece of duct tape over his mouth.

Chad crept along the hallway toward the cave entrance. He didn't know whether Keeva and Two Feathers had succeeded in getting through the compound and into the cave. Chad wasn't certain what he would encounter, but he had to try to reach them if they were still alive. Chad heard two men coming down the hallway. He darted into an open doorway and hid behind a cabinet just inside the room. He heard the men talking. One said, "Mr. Parker wants us to check on the prisoners. He's coming to interrogate them some more."

The second man replied, "Do you think that Mr. Parker is going to have them killed?"

The first man laughed. "Yes, and I suspect we're the ones who will have to do the duty."

Chad knew then that he could not let the men reach the holding cells. They would see that the prisoners had been released and would sound the alarm. He stepped out quickly behind the men and called to them. "Parker wants you to return to the cabin."

The men turned around in bewilderment. As the men turned, Chad threw a flying side kick with his leg to the man on the left and a simultaneous twisting front kick with his other leg to the man on the right. Both men staggered under the blows. Chad quickly assessed which man was likely to recover first and followed with a hard blow to the rib cage that knocked him against the wall. Chad executed a back kick to the other man who jumped into the kick trying to get to Chad. Both men collapsed to the floor unconscious. Chad dragged both men into the empty room and quickly tied them with some nylon strapping he found on some shelves. He then put packing tape over their mouths. He didn't want any early warnings to the compound that something was amiss.

Chad continued down the corridor to the entrance. As he approached the entrance, Chad saw two men standing there in the sunlight. The sunlight produced shadows covering the men's features, so he was not able to determine the identity of the men. He decided to play it safe and called to them. "Hi, there. How's it going?"

"Not so good. Parker and his men are coming this way,"

Keeva answered, confirming his identity to Chad. "We have no choice but to find another way out."

"Okay. Come on. We'll catch up to the others if we can," Chad said.

Keeva and Two Feathers stepped back into the shadows of the cave and away from the entrance. When they were well out of the sunlight, they turned, picked up their bows, and ran to Chad. All three continued quickly down the hallway. When they reached the first bend, they stopped and leaned against the wall, listening to see if Parker and his men were in pursuit.

Parker and four men entered the cave. "Hey, where are the guards?" Parker said. He motioned for his men to spread out and to go ahead to check out the corridor. All of the men pulled out guns. They came to the first room and found the guards lying on the floor. Parker was furious. "We have to get to the prisoners. We don't want anyone to escape."

Parker and his men started down the corridor. Keeva and Two Feathers lifted their bows and let two arrows fly. Two men dropped instantly. One man was hit in the chest. The other was hit in the shoulder. Gunshots echoed loudly down the cave hallways. Chad, Keeva, and Two Feathers dropped back. Parker and his men found cover and continued firing in their direction. Chad had his gun out but had not fired it. The three of them sprinted down the corridor, past the holding cells and onwards toward the narrow crevice that they hoped would be their escape route. A man jumped out from a room along the corridor and pointed his gun at the three coming his way. As he cocked the hammer, all three went into a flying somersault. The gun discharged sending a bullet harmlessly above the three men. Chad, in front, recovered from his somersault and threw a flying scissor kick to the man, smashing his nose and knocking him unconscious.

Elice jumped uncontrollably when she heard the gunshots. She thought quickly of Chad, then focused on the task at hand. "*Come on!* We have to hurry. This way."

They hurried as fast as they could. They came to the crevice that led to the outside on the other side of the mountain. All of them were able to squeeze through the crevice. Jasper had the most trouble owing to his head injury, which greatly weakened him. They worked their way along the narrow passageway and eventually came to the narrow ledge at the outside entrance.

Chad and his comrades came to the crevice with Parker's men not too far behind. Keeva and Two Feathers went through the crevice with Chad close behind. Chad waited to let Keeva and Two Feathers get a good start. He shot his .44 Magnum down the corridor to hold off Parker's men. The sound was deafening and temporarily silenced the guns of Parker's men. Chad squinted from the safety of the crevice and only saw two men. He didn't see Parker. He surmised that Parker had returned to the compound to get help. With that, Chad fired once more and quickly turned and followed Keeva and Two Feathers down the narrow passageway.

"Chad?" Elice asked as she saw only the two Indians. "*Chad!*" she exclaimed when she saw Chad rush out of the passageway.

Dave surveyed the situation, noting the precipitous drop from the ledge and the insurmountable rock face above them. "What's our next move?"

"We're ad-libbing from this point on. I think we should go down, and not up," Chad replied.

"Okay, how do we do that?" Dave asked.

Chad looked at the two ropes still tied to the ledge. They both hung below the ledge about half the distance to the valley floor — not enough to safely drop without injury. "I'll go up to cut one of the ropes. You pull up the other one to tie the two ends together. Hopefully, that will give us enough line to reach the bottom."

Two Feathers spoke up for the first time. "I will climb up. I can go faster."

Chad could not help but notice his muscular upper body and nodded.

Two Feathers strung his bow over his shoulder, checked the gun in his belt, and began to quickly climb one of the ropes. He made good time and reached the top quickly. He motioned to Chad to grab hold and then cut one of the ropes. Then Two Feathers disappeared from sight of those below him.

Chad called to him to come down. Keeva gently told Chad

that he was not coming back. "Where is he going?" Chad asked.

"Two Feathers will buy us time if Parker sends men to the top of the mountain. Parker certainly knows our escape route is to the other side of the mountain from his compound. We can't let them cut the rope and prevent our escape." Keeva walked to the ledge and looked down. "Now we must go. Two Feathers' effort must not be in vain." With that Keeva stabilized the rope and motioned for Elice to go down first.

Elice and Kat went one after another. Dave went next. The three of them reached the bottom without incident. When Dave reached the bottom, they heard shots from the top of the ridge. Several shots were fired. Yet, as long as the gunshots sounded, they knew that Two Feathers was still alive.

Jasper was next to climb and had some trouble. However, he managed to reach the bottom unharmed. Joslyn was more timid with the climb downward, but understood the alternative to not climbing. As Joslyn was descending, both Chad and Keeva fired into the passageway to stop the men from advancing any farther. The two men who had followed them had been joined by others. Chad and Keeva's shots hit one man who turned slightly to the front and provided an effective wedge in the narrow passageway.

Keeva immediately grabbed the rope and swung out over the ledge. Chad did not wait but an instant and followed Keeva. The weight of the two of them on the rope at the same time put a tremendous strain on the line. They both scrambled down the line, one after the other. They were about five meters from the bottom when the rope broke at the top. Keeva and Chad tumbled the rest of the way to the bottom. They lay there for a moment, both stunned. Kat and Elice ran to them to help them. Dave stared at the top of the ridge far upward. The gunshots had stopped. Soon, men appeared at the ridge, looking down at them. Others appeared at the ledge to the passageway and shouted to them to stop.

"Come on! We gotta find cover," Dave shouted as he started pulling Jasper into the nearby brush. The others followed as bullets whizzed by them from the men above.

Dave, Keeva, and Chad fired at the men on the ledge to push them back. The men on the ridge were firing at them as well. The men on the ridge were too far up for shots to reach them from the valley.

The fugitives moved through the underbrush to get away from the rock face. They knew it was only a matter of time before the men would find a way down. They hurried away from the mountain and picked their way through the brush.

They filed through the underbrush as quietly as possible. Keeva was leading the way. Suddenly he motioned for everyone to be quiet. He had heard something or someone coming towards them. Dave and Chad moved off to either side of Keeva to surprise whoever or whatever was coming. The others dropped to the ground to remain as invisible as possible. They heard footsteps as a man came through the brush towards them. Chad, Keeva, and Dave rose at the same time and confronted the man who appeared from behind a bush. The man started to yell, but held his voice. Dave was the first to speak. "*Trapper*! You scared us."

"Scared you? I almost had a heart attack," Trapper exclaimed.

Kat came up and hugged him. "I thought you had been killed."

"I thought I had, too," Trapper replied, dryly.

Chad changed the subject. "Which way do you think we should go?"

Trapper nodded behind him. "I wouldn't be surprised if some of those men start looking this way for me. They know by now that the person starting the fire did it as a distraction. I think we should go this way." He pointed to the south.

As Chad looked to the south, he couldn't help but think of Two Feathers and his sacrifice for the others. "Why do life's choices have to be so complicated?" he thought.

Chapter 21

Escape

The going was rough. Jasper and Trapper were still suffering from their injuries. None of them had had any food for several hours. The stress and the physical exertion of the escape was taking a toll on all of them. The merciless sun would not set in Alaska at this time of the year. So, with no darkness, they would have to be extra careful.

Dave was leading now. He knew the area about as well as anyone. Chad was close behind Dave. The others followed, with Keeva bringing up the rear. Keeva would occasionally drop behind, then would suddenly reappear. This indicated to Chad that either the party was moving slower than he thought, or Keeva was tireless. Perhaps it was a little of both.

Chad expected that Parker would mount a massive search effort. It would probably come from two or three directions. One search party would follow along the same path they had taken. The second would come cross-country from where Trapper had started the fire. The third would probably come from a group of men sent down the access road as far as it could go, who would then turn inward. Chad hoped that Parker did not have a helicopter.

As they walked, Chad asked Dave some questions. "Dave, I have Kat's cell phone, which she left at camp. We could call for help. However, do you know who we could call – who wouldn't sound the alarm to Parker? And, also, do you know much about Parker?"

"Let me answer the second question first." Dave said as he picked his way through the underbrush. "I don't know that much about Parker, except he's been here all his life and is in charge of the logging being done by the Dena'ina. And, now we know he has been doing some illegal placer mining. He has been rather reclusive and not well known to the general populace. However, I know he has a lot of influence around here, because he owns a lot of property. Many folks who have stores in Soldotna somehow have a connection to Parker, or at least know of him. I know some of his men — none of whom are very reputable. I have had to arrest some of them in the past. Some have seen my jail frequently."

"What about the state police? Do they know him, or have a file on him?" Chad asked.

"That is curious," Dave mused. "I know that at one point when I had three of his men in jail, I tried to check on what the State Police had on Parker. There wasn't a file. Or, the person I talked to wasn't cooperating. I don't know which. I didn't think much of it at the time. However, now I wonder."

"Well, with that uncertainty, maybe we shouldn't use the phone just yet," Chad said.

"Right," Dave replied.

They were steadily climbing and soon reached the top of a ridge. Chad ordered a rest. While Elice and Joslyn checked on Trapper and Jasper, the others searched for higher ground that would give them a view of where they had come. Kat was the first to see a small band of men in the east winding their way along the same path the fugitives had just come. Keeva thought he saw a second band further to the south and coming from the access road across the valley. Dave was searching to the north and the west to get his bearings on which way to go.

"It's only a matter of time before they catch up with us," Chad said to no one in particular, as he watched the small band coming up the trail. "We need a plan."

Dave returned to where Chad was standing. "I see where we need to go — straight west. I would say we are about a day away from a trail I know will lead us back to Soldotna."

Chad kept watching the band of men. "What if we were to go south to the access road? I don't think they would be expecting us to do that. Besides, we will not be able to remain ahead of them for a whole day."

"But, the second band of men is coming from that direction," Kat said.

"I know. But, I think we should try. Hopefully, with the element of surprise, we can take them. Once we get to the road, it will be easier going."

"What if Parker has more men waiting for us?" Kat asked.

"I know it's a risk. But, look at Trapper and Jasper. They're not up to a strenuous hike through the wilderness, even if they are the most woods-savvy of any of us. Besides, Hilary said that he was sending some help. They won't be able to find us way out there." Chad motioned behind him to the west.

Keeva stepped up to them. "Chad's idea may work." Keeva looked at Chad. "You and Dave continue along this rocky ridge and leave sign as if a larger party is coming through. Do this for a few miles before you double back. The first band of men may lose us that way. I will lead the others along the path toward the access road. I will leave them in a safe place while I go ahead and scout how many men are in the band in front of us."

"Okay, but I'm not sure this is a good idea," Kat mumbled as she went to help Elice and Joslyn with the injured men.

Keeva led the party along the ridge, sticking to the rocky ground. They continued in this direction until the path turned west. This is where Chad and Dave would part from the others. The two men watched the small party begin doubling back, paralleling the ridge, but lower down the side of the hill. Chad and Dave then turned in the direction they had been going to follow the ridgeline to the west for an hour before descending from the rocky ridge into the brush. Using Trapper's machete, they hacked a trail through the brush. They continued this for about a half mile when they came to a clearing. They hoped this would confuse Parker's men for a while. Chad and Dave turned back and hurried as fast as they could back to the ridge from which they had descended. They picked their way along the base of the hill, following where Keeva had led the others. They came upon a red bandana that Keeva had left on a bush. Retrieving the bandana, Chad and Dave carefully entered the brush, trying not to disturb any vegetation.

It did not take Chad and Dave too long to catch up with the others. They were moving slower, partly because of fatigue, and partly because they were now between two bands of Parker's men who were searching for them. They finally came to a clump of trees that provided some shelter from any observation. Keeva said, "Why don't you rest here. I'll scout ahead. I think we're three or four hours away from the second band. That should give all of you time to rest."

Before anyone could say anything, Keeva was gone.

Joslyn, Trapper, and Jasper didn't need any more encouragement to take a rest. They curled up on the ground right where they were and were soon asleep.

Elice sat down next to Chad. "You know, it seems whenever you and I are in the wilderness together, some bad men are around."

Chad smiled. "You're right. I don't think it's you. It seems my field trips are always becoming this exciting. I'm beginning to realize that more than a few of PERI's projects include a certain element of danger." Chad's look changed to sadness. "I *am* sorry that you have gotten caught up in this. I don't want anything to happen to you."

Elice touched his arm. "You must know by now that I want to be here. Besides, my field trips haven't been without their danger. It's hard to be anywhere in the wilderness of Alaska without some element of danger."

Dave and Kat joined them. "What are you two talking about?"

Chad said, "Oh, we were just talking about the amount of danger that always seems to follow us around."

Dave said, "Yes, this field survey has turned out to be more dangerous than most of the situations I encounter as a police officer back in Soldotna. But, I can't say that I am sorry I came. Maybe I should wait a while longer before I say that." He smiled at Kat. She smiled back.

"You know," Kat said as she turned to look at Chad. "I seem to remember a few exciting field trips with you in the past."

Chad smiled. "It has been a long time since we were in the field together."

Kat gave Chad a serious look. "I'm still not sure why Sir Hilary didn't tell either of us that we were on separate surveys in the same area. Do you know?"

Chad thought for a moment about Kat's question before answering. "I think I understand it better now. I didn't at the time. I don't think either Hilary or Hodges wanted us to team up, because they knew there was a high probability that I would be attracting some danger. I don't think they expected you would be in the same area. If the bear had not attacked Don, and you had continued with your survey farther to the northwest, you would not have been in a position to run into me. However, once you had to abort your original plan, you saw the opportunity to sample streams in a different area, which is where my survey was planned. So, I don't think they were malicious, but trying to be more strategic with the two surveys. I think they really thought they were going to get two independent assessments of what was going on here on the Kenai Peninsula. If we came up with the same answer, they would be validated in their suspicions."

"I guess you're right," Kat said. "It makes sense. However, it still would have been great to have coordinated our efforts."

Chad dozed without being in a full sleep. He would wake frequently whenever he heard an unusual noise. He heard Keeva return to their makeshift camp. Chad was up as Keeva walked into the camp. "They're coming this way," Keeva said. "They don't know we're here. I believe they're in communication with the first band, so they know the location of each other."

"That means that we must either let them pass unseen, or surprise them before they can call the others," Chad thought out loud.

Keeva thought about that. "I do not think we will be able to hide from them to let them pass. We won't have much cover to avoid them. And, I think they would detect us if we try to get around them."

"How many men?" Chad asked.

"There are five men. Two of them are the ones who came into your camp and fought the others." Keeva replied.

Dave joined them. "It sounds like Fred and Bubb are with the band."

The others were up now and had heard some of the conversation. They had gotten almost three hours of sleep. "What about you Keeva? Did you get any rest?" Joslyn asked.

"I got some while I waited for the men. They're really tired, themselves. They're arguing with each other, and not even trying to keep quiet. I think they believe we're far away."

"In that case, I think we should surprise them. What do the

rest of you think?" Chad asked.

Dave spoke first. "I agree. I don't think we should let them by."

"If they're in communication with the other band of men, what happens when they don't call in?" Kat asked.

"Hopefully, we will have a pretty good head start. I think that this is a better option than letting both groups catch up with us," Chad replied.

"I say we better get going, then," Elice said.

The tired party followed Keeva as he led them toward a place where he thought an ambush would work for them. The place that Keeva had selected was near a stream and with a very rocky landscape. Large boulders loomed overhead and lined the banks of the stream. The vegetation was sparse, but with the large boulders, the passage was made more difficult. Chad nodded in approval. This place offered them an escape route that could be defended easily by one man, if need be. The men would have to come from the cover of the bushes on the opposite side of the stream, cross a small meadow before reaching the stream, then make their way through the boulders on this side. The rocky area afforded substantial hiding places for them.

Chad and Keeva positioned everyone in their places and crouched down to wait. It didn't take long. Soon, the first of the band emerged from the bushes across the stream. It was Fred.

Bubb was the second man to come into the meadow. Fred

and Bubb stopped and seemed to be talking and pointing in their direction.

Chad wondered if they knew they were there. He became nervous that somehow the men knew their location. If they didn't have the element of surprise, then the whole party would be in serious danger.

Eventually, the other three men joined Fred and Bubb. They continued on toward the stream. Chad breathed a sigh. They must not discover his group of tired fugitives.

As the men came onward, Fred and Bubb were now bringing up the rear and still talking. At least Fred was talking, and Bubb was listening. As they approached, Chad could barely make out the conversation above the sound of the flowing stream and an eagle screeching above them.

"I tell you. If we don't get them, Parker will have our heads," Fred was saying. "He is furious. Butch and his men will overtake them soon, I hope. By the time we get there, it'll be all over. But, Parker isn't taking any chances. He's leading another group of men to intercept them if they get by Butch and us."

Bubb took this opportunity to make one of his brief statements. "We will get them."

"Yah, well, we better do it soon. I'm really tired," Fred replied.

When the last of them entered the stream to wade across, the first was just reaching the side where Chad and the others were hidden. That was when Chad came out from hiding with his gun drawn. "Howdy. I guess you're all wondering what I'm doing here."

The men looked up. The first man who had reached the bank automatically began to raise his rifle. Chad turned toward him. "I wouldn't do that –"

Before he could finish his sentence, an arrow flew from Keeva's bow and struck the man holding the gun in his side. The man dropped his gun, clutched his side and fell. The others stopped where they were.

"Anybody else have a problem?" Chad asked. "Now, come on out of there."

As the men came out of the water, Keeva, Dave, Kat, and Elice emerged from their cover. Joslyn stayed with Trapper and Jasper. Keeva had put down his bow and had his gun out, as did Dave. Elice had the gun that Chad had taken off the man in the cave. Kat had no weapon. They all surrounded the men as they exited the water and stood on the bank.

"Drop your guns," Chad ordered.

Elice was standing closest to Bubb. She inadvertently had left the safety on her pistol, and she wasn't in a position to get a shot off.

The men hesitated in following Chad's order. That moment of hesitation was enough to add confusion to the situation. Before she could stop him, Bubb moved like lightning and grabbed Elice's gun hand and pulled her toward him. He twisted her, so he had her around the neck with her back to him and lightly lifted her off the ground. He used her as a shield and wrested the gun from her hand. Bubb started to remove the safety as he was bringing the gun up. Kat moved in that split second. She jumped low toward Bubb as a base runner would slide into base. Kat brought her foot up into a kick driven directly at Bubb's crotch and between Elice's legs, which were spread as she struggled in mid-air against Bubb's tight grasp. Bubb exhaled sharply at the impact and dropped Elice immediately. Elice hit the ground and rolled while Bubb fell hard in the place where she had been. Kat was there to give Bubb a sharp knifehand hit to the back of his neck. Bubb lost consciousness.

As Chad's eyes were momentarily diverted to Bubb and Elice, the man in front of him brought his rifle up and hit Chad's arm, making him release his pistol. Then the man used the butt of his rifle to ram Chad's shoulder hard, sending him spinning. Keeva and Dave moved toward the men in front of them. Keeva quickly dispatched his man with an open hand strike against the rifle of the man, knocking the barrel into his face. He then swung his pistol across the back of the man's head to knock him unconscious.

Dave confronted Fred who ducked under a swing and launched a series of punches into Dave's side. Fred was quite wiry for his small size. However, Dave recovered and swung a backfist that caught Fred in the temple. This made Fred stagger, and Dave followed with a hard downward punch that sent Fred to the ground.

After knocking Chad down, the man turned and stepped

toward Keeva, training his rifle on Keeva's back as he finished off his man. At this distance, the man would not miss. Suddenly, the man flew head over heels in a sidewise somersault, his rifle flying from his hand. Chad and Kat had seen the impending situation and had simultaneously reached the man from different directions. They had leapt into the air in synchrony each throwing a flying kick. Kat's scissor kick connected with the rifle flinging it high in the air, while Chad's flying side kick hit the man in his side. The force and momentum sent the man into a tailspin. He was unconscious before he hit the ground.

With all the men unconscious, the fugitives sat down and caught their breath. No one said anything for a moment. Then, they heard a voice. "Fred, come in. Come in." Chad located the walkie-talkie, still attached to Fred's belt. The voice continued. "Fred, come in. We have turned around. We think they doubled back. Fred, come in."

Chad picked up the walkie-talkie, but before he could speak, Dave took it from him. "I know Fred and think I can imitate his voice. Let me try."

Chad gladly let Dave take the walkie-talkie. Dave took out his shirttail and held it over the speaker, rubbing the fabric over the plastic covering of the speaker, making a static sound. He pushed the button and spoke. "I'm here. Hold your horses."

"You're breaking up. You sound far away," The voice on the other end said

"Yah, I dropped the walkie-talkie. What's up?" Dave asked.

The voice accepted that. "We think they turned around and may be coming your way. We're coming that way now. We found some signs that they passed this way. Anyway, we think it's them. So keep your eyes peeled. We should meet up with you soon."

"Okay, we'll watch for them. Over and out," Dave said and turned off the walkie-talkie. He looked at Chad.

"We better get going. Let's tie these men over there behind the boulders. Hopefully, they won't be found by the other band coming this way," Chad said.

As soon as they had the men tied and hidden, they set out at a fast a pace. They knew they had some distance to go before they reached the access road. Chad also wondered where Parker was and which way he would be coming. He hoped that they hadn't just gotten into a deeper predicament than before. Chad glanced back at his rag-tag group. "What a great group," he thought. "I can't let them down!"

Chapter 22

The Storm

After five hours of hiking and only about three hours of rest in a day and a half, they were all very tired. They had gone several miles, despite the injuries and lack of sleep. Chad looked at Keeva and noted the weariness in the warrior. Yes, they had to rest. Chad surveyed the area and saw a clump of trees on a little knoll. That should be a good place for us to rest, he thought. He turned to the others. "Let's take a few minutes to recuperate. Over there looks like a good place." He received no objection from the others. Chad said he would take the first watch.

Chad caught himself dozing. Dave rose from the ground and came up to him. "It's my turn, Chad," he said. "You take a little rest, yourself. I'll wake you if anything comes up." Chad didn't argue.

Chad awoke with a start. How long had he been sleeping? he wondered. Keeva was sitting on a rock with his back to him. He must have been sleeping through at least one shift change. What time was it? He checked his watch. He had slept for about three hours. He looked around at his colleagues sleeping peacefully on the ground around the area.

"Keeva, how are you doing? Have you seen anything?" Chad asked as he stretched.

Keeva pointed to the trees on the horizon. "The men who have been following us just appeared from over the ridge. It is time for us to go."

Chad took one more look at his colleagues, still deep in sleep. "Okay, gang! Let's get ourselves together. It's time to leave. We have a bunch of bad guys on our heels." Chad walked over to Jasper and Trapper. They were doing much better, having had some sleep. He was glad they had taken some of the food and water from Fred and his band. Chad broke out the rations. After everyone had eaten a little bit and had some water, they were much more refreshed.

They were all in better spirits as they traipsed through the wilderness toward the unknown. They knew where they were going — just didn't know what they would find. Chad and Keeva knew what was behind them, and knew they couldn't turn back..

They could see the storm coming toward them. The dense black and gray clouds looked ominous. The mountain peak ahead of them quickly disappeared in the thick blanket of dark clouds and torrential downpour.

Chad looked at Keeva. "Shelter?" was all he said.

"Not sure." Keeva scanned the landscape to the east. The storm was coming from the south – the direction they wanted to go. "Let's go that way," he pointed.

Chad could see the terrain rise into a small hill. Perhaps in the more hilly terrain there would be shelter.

The rag-tag group hurried as quickly as they could toward the distant hill. Keeva ran ahead while Chad herded his tired group through the underbrush.

Within an hour, they were in the rocky terrain of the hill. The vegetation was low growing and sparse. Rocky outcrops and large boulders were strewn upon the hillside in no particular fashion. Keeva was nowhere to be seen.

"This way," Chad said, directing the others toward a trio of large boulders clumped in a straight line facing the south. Perhaps they could all huddle behind the boulders until the storm passed.

Before they could reach the boulders, the storm was upon

them. The tremendous wind sounded like a locomotive as the downpour pelted against the rock and vegetation. Within seconds they were all drenched. The combination of dark clouds and dense rain hampered visibility. Chad could barely see the blurry outline of Joslyn at the end of the line of people and could not see Jasper who was behind her.

Chad reached the boulders and ducked behind them where the force of the storm was lessened somewhat. He saw that a large slab of rock had broken off one of the boulders and had fallen off forming a crude lean-to. Luck was with them.

"Come on, there's shelter here," Chad shouted against the wind.

One by one, the soaked fugitives came around the boulders – all except Jasper.

"Where's Jasper?" Chad asked Joslyn as she turned the corner.

Joslyn looked behind her. "I don't know. I thought he was with us."

Chad peered through the dense rain. "All of you stay here. I'm going to find Jasper."

The others crowded under the lean-to, which only served to block the ferociousness of the storm. The rain and wind still seeped through the cracks and the open end of the rocky shelter.

Chad walked against the force of the wind back the way they had come. "*Jasper,*" he shouted.

No answer.

He walked further, squinting against the pouring rain. He was now uncertain of being on the path they had just traversed. He stopped and listened. The wind was too fierce to hear anything else. "*Jasper.*"

"Here," came a faint reply.

"Where, Jasper? Keep talking."

"I'm here, beside a rock," Jasper said.

Chad could see the faint outline of Jasper sitting on the ground and leaning against a rock. Chad knelt down when he reached Jasper. "Are you okay?"

"Yes, I just needed to rest. I lost sight of Joslyn and thought it best I waited here until the storm cleared."

"Come on," Chad said. "Lets go to where the others are. They are in a shelter of sorts. Can you stand?"

"Yes, just help me up."

Together, they hobbled up the hill toward the boulders. When they reached the shelter, the others moved to allow Jasper to squeeze in the tight space. Arms reached out to Jasper to help him sit in the small opening they had created. There wasn't enough room for Chad, so he sat on the outside leaning inwards to get his head in out of the rain.

"Where is Keeva?" Dave asked.

"I don't know. He is most likely holed up somewhere nearby to wait out the storm. He was going to find shelter for the rest of us,

243

but the storm came in too quickly." Chad shifted his weight to get more comfortable.

"I'm hungry," Joslyn said to no one in particular.

Yes, they hadn't eaten much over the past few days. Chad thought about where he was going to find food and how he was going to get it.

The storm lasted for only a few hours. As the darkness lifted and the clouds moved on, the sun's warmth revived the wet and weary fugitives. They came out from the shelter and stretched to relieve the stiffness they all felt from the cramped quarters. Chad thought it was late evening – it's so hard to tell when the sun doesn't set at night.

Chad looked at his surroundings. Let's spread out to find Keeva. Don't go far, though. We don't want anyone else lost. Joslyn, do you mind staying with Trapper and Jasper? They look really tired."

"Okay," Joslyn said.

Before they had moved a few paces, Keeva rounded the hill and waved.

"*Keeva*," Kat shouted. Everyone turned and looked where she pointed.

"I see you were able to get out of the storm," Keeva said as he surveyed the crude rock slab the others used for their shelter. "I'm sorry I couldn't get back to you soon enough."

Chad looked at Keeva. "You're dry. You must have found a

better shelter."

"Yes, and I'm going to take you there now. I found a small cave – well, it's really a cut-away under a rock ledge. There was a clump of fallen tree branches nearby that I threw in the shelter before I set out to find you. I have a fire going."

"You came out looking for us?" Elice asked.

"Yes, but before I got very far, the storm hit. I saw a deer trying to outrun the storm. It stopped when it saw me. That's all the time I needed to stick an arrow into its heart. I dragged it back to the shelter and cleaned it. I was hoping all the time that you were all coming around the hill in my direction. As the storm continued, I figured you would have taken whatever shelter you could find."

Chad looked at the shelter he had found. "Well, it wasn't much, but it made us a little more comfortable than being out in the full brunt of the storm."

"Now that I have found you, let me feed you. The meat should be about done now."

The fugitives didn't need any more encouragement. Dave and Chad helped Trapper and Jasper.

Keeva led the way to the cave where the smell of cooking venison wafted through the air. The overhanging ledge interrupted the flow of smoke enough that a tell-tale plume would not visible unless someone was looking specifically for it.

Chad hadn't realized how hungry he had gotten. He looked around at the others eating eagerly and concentrating on their food.

After they had eaten, even Trapper and Jasper looked like they had regained some of their strength. Kat was the first to speak. "Keeva, I think this is the best venison I have ever tasted."

"Its probably because you were just hungry. It was a small deer, so was quite tender, wasn't it?"

"Yes, it was," Joslyn chimed in.

Chad crawled out from the cave and stood up. "I would bet our pursuers are also holed up somewhere. However, they will be coming soon. We better get going."

Keeva and Dave put out the fire and scattered the remains of their dinner for the wolves and other scavengers who would not be far away. The fugitives gathered themselves and set out once more for who knows where. Their spirits were lifted with food in their stomachs and nearly dry clothes from the fire and warm sun.

Chapter 23

Retribution

Chad and Kat were walking together at the rear of the party. Keeva and Jasper were leading. Chad turned to Kat. "I think I'm going to try the cell phone and call Don. It may not be that much of a risk now, because the other band of men knows by now what we are trying to do. I suspect they have already tried to call Parker."

"Yah, I think you're right. Go ahead and call. I'm sure he's worried to death, wondering what is happening out here."

Chad pulled out the cell phone and dialed the number to the hospital.

"Hello, hello," Don said, anxiously.

"Hello, Don. I can't talk long," Chad said quickly. "This line may be monitored. We are all okay. Kat is right here with me. We are trying to make our escape from Parker. I need you to call this number." He gave Don the number of PERI. "Ask for either Sir Hilary or Senator Hodges. Tell them we are making our way out of the wilderness going south toward the access road of the compound and that we are being followed by some of Parker's men. We need help." And, then as an afterthought, Chad added, "Also tell them that Congressman Masserman is one of the good guys, okay?"

"Okay. Do you want me to call the police?" Don asked.

"No. We aren't sure who we can trust. Parker has long tentacles in this part of the Kenai. And, don't tell anyone at the hospital just yet. Okay?"

"I understand," Don said, and then added, "I wish there was something more I could do."

"You've been a big help, Don. We'll be in touch." Chad turned off the phone.

Dave dropped back to where Chad and Kat were. "I think I know someone in the state police we can trust. Let me try to reach them."

Chad looked at Kat, then at Dave. "Okay, but if someone else answers, hang up. We aren't in a good position to let our guard down now."

Dave took the phone from Chad and dialed a number. "Hello Helen. It's Dave."

"Dave! I've been worried about you. Where are you?" Helen asked.

"I'll have to fill you in later. Is Johnson available? I need to talk to him."

"Yes, but he just walked into a meeting. Can I leave him a message?" Helen asked.

"No, I can't wait that long. Could you ask him if he could talk to me for a minute?"

Helen put him on hold, and she checked with Todd Johnson. It was a full two minutes before Johnson was able to pick up the phone. "Hello, Dave. What's going on?"

"Listen, Todd. I need your help. Do you know much about Johann Parker?" Dave asked.

"Why yes," Johnson answered. "He runs the logging operation for the Dena'ina. His men seem to get into a lot of trouble."

"Yes, that's him," Dave said. "He's also doing some illegal mining activities, and, he's guilty of kidnapping. Right now, we're trying to escape from him."

"What do you mean — escape?" Johnson asked.

"I don't have time to explain fully. Our phone line might be monitored." Dave was talking quickly. "You may be the only one we can trust. We don't know whether Parker has penetrated the police department and has any of the officers on his payroll. I know that sounds weird, but right now, we're desperate and don't want to take any chances."

"You hang tight," Johnson said. "I will come get you with a helicopter. Be watching for us. I'll look for you on the access road."

Dave turned off the cell phone and retracted the antenna. "Johnson is going to send a helicopter to get us. Once we get to the access road, they'll be able to find us quickly."

"How did he know we were going for the access road?" Chad asked.

"Oh, no!" Dave exclaimed, as the realization set in.

They were steadily climbing, and finally reached the access road. They scanned the road and surrounding area carefully before coming out of the brush. As Chad reached the road, he saw Keeva staring in the direction from which they came. Chad looked to see what he was observing. The men had gained on them. Chad could see that the men were getting closer. He saw one of the men point to them. They had been seen.

Chad darted up the road toward the compound, shouting for the others to follow. They only went about a hundred meters, which put them out of sight behind some trees beside the road. Keeva watched carefully as the men passed them and disappeared from

250

view. "Okay, they're out of sight," Keeva said.

Chad then told everyone to change direction and go down the road, away from the compound. He was hoping their change of direction would fake out the men once they reached the road.

The party of fugitives crouched and ran down the road, trying to keep to the shadows. Keeva and Chad were slightly ahead of the others when they rounded a turn in the road and detected two jeeps blocking the road, about thirty meters away. Four men were standing on the other side of the jeeps and looking out into the bush. Their backs were to Chad and Keeva and the men didn't see them as they stopped short and dove behind a boulder beside the road. Chad and Keeva motioned to the others to hold up.

Chad and Keeva watched the four men by the jeep for a few minutes. The men all had rifles, and seemed to be intent on something going on in the wilderness. "I think another band of men is making its way into the wilderness and is looking for us. Those men must be guards watching the jeeps," Keeva said.

"I think you're right. We have to get by them. I don't see how we are going to avoid a confrontation, do you?" Chad asked.

"No, I don't think so," Keeva replied. "Besides, we could use those jeeps."

Chad motioned to Keeva and they backed away from their positions. Once they were back around the bend with the others, they construed a strategy to confront the men. It was a simple plan.

Kat and Elice crept carefully along the road on the opposite side of the road where the men were looking. The cover was negligible here. The women had to be careful not to be seen. Meanwhile, Chad, Keeva, and Dave filed quietly through the brush alongside the road on the same side as the guards. When Chad and the other men were within five meters of the jeeps, they stopped and waited.

Kat and Elice took their time reaching the jeeps. When they were within a few meters of the jeep, they crouched and watched for an opportunity. The opportunity came soon enough and the women quietly approached the back of one of the jeeps, still in a crouched position. They remained crouched behind the jeep, and Kat took time to let her hair down from the loose ponytail she had kept it in. She ran her fingers through her hair to try to smooth it out. The blond hair shimmered in the sunlight. She unbuttoned the top two buttons of her safari shirt. She motioned to Elice to do the same. Then they were ready. They stood up and walked from behind the jeep, and Kat said, "Heh! You there. Can you help us?"

The men swiveled quickly at the sound of her voice and gawked at the sight of the two beautiful women standing there, one leaning against the jeep in a position that made her shirt open slightly and the other standing with legs apart and hands on hips, the shirt gaping open.

"What the ... what are you doing here ...?" One man stammered, keeping his eyes locked on Elice's chest.

As the women were distracting the men, Chad, Keeva, and

Dave came out of the brush. Chad and Keeva leapt over the jeeps, throwing side kicks into two of the men who were just turning at the sound of the commotion. Dave ran between the jeeps and dove into a third man who was swinging his rifle around. Kat covered the short distance to the men and threw a sweep kick at the knees of the fourth man, knocking him swiftly to the ground and making him lose his rifle. Kat rolled in a forward motion and punched the man in the throat.

Chad and Keeva both connected with their targets at the same time, giving the impression that they had choreographed their moves prior to the ambush. Their side kicks to the temples of the men knocked them unconscious immediately. Dave knocked his man down and was on top of him before the man could resist. Dave landed two punches to the man's face in quick succession.

In a matter of seconds, the four guards were all taken out of commission. Elice motioned to Joslyn, Jasper, and Trapper to join them quickly. As they all congregated at the jeep, a band of men led by Parker came out of the brush. The encounter surprised everyone on both sides. In the split second of confusion, the fugitives took the initiative to attack. Although Jasper and Trapper were still not fully recovered, they entered the fray as well. Jasper found himself face to face with Parker. Parker smiled at Jasper as he took a swing at the Indian. However, he underestimated the quickness of the old Indian. Jasper ducked under the swing and retaliated with a hard fist to Parker's kidneys. Parker winced with pain, recovered, and threw a backfist at Jasper. The Indian moved back to avoid the fist, then moved in again with another fist to Parker's throat. Parker doubled with new pain mixed with the old. Jasper kicked upward to snap Parker's head back. Parker collapsed to the ground unconscious.

The fugitives outnumbered Parker's men, mostly because the four guards had been eliminated earlier. However, the group did not escape injury. Dave's shoulder was slashed with a knife. Trapper's wound was re-opened, and a new knife wound was on his arm. Fortunately, no one had been shot.

When it was over, Chad checked out his crew. Everyone was alive, though bruised and battered. Dave's and Trapper's injuries were not life threatening. Chad saw Jasper standing over Parker. He walked over to the Indian and stood there for a moment, watching him as he inwardly struggled with a difficult decision.

After a few moments, Jasper looked up at Chad. "I know this man was not responsible for what happened to my ancestors. But, he has lied and deceived my people. He should not live."

"Jasper," Chad replied. "Let the authorities take care of Parker."

"The authorities will do nothing," Jasper said, scornfully.

"Dave is a police officer and a good man," Chad argued. "He will see that justice is served."

"Yes, I will, Jasper," Dave said as he approached the two men. "You can count on me."

Jasper looked at Dave, then at Chad. "I trust you. But, this must not be forgotten." Jasper turned without another word and walked away.

Dave looked at Chad. "I guess he's putting a pretty weighty responsibility on us, isn't he?"

"Do you blame him?" Chad replied. "There are a couple of generations of pain built up in him. He now has the answers and is in a position to serve retribution. He's trusting us to make it complete."

Chapter 24

Retreat

The jeeps careened down the access road going away from the compound. Chad was driving the first jeep, and Elice the second. There was a temporary sense of calm among the group as they got further away from Parker's compound. However, Chad and Elice were still driving with a sense of urgency.

As they came around a bend in the road, they entered a clearing and a dip in the ridgeline that had been paralleling the road up to this point. Suddenly a helicopter rose above the ridge and turned in their direction. Chad slowed as the helicopter approached.

Besides the pilot, two other men were in the chopper. Dave immediately recognized Todd Johnson, the state police officer he had called earlier. When Johnson saw Dave in the jeep, he pulled out a rifle and took aim.

Chad could see the alarm in Dave's eyes. He recovered quickly and shouted to Chad. "Let's get outta here. He's going to shoot." Chad floored the jeep with Elice right behind. The jeeps jumped along the road, which led out of the clearing and into some low trees.

This action was enough to forestall any shooting. The helicopter climbed over the treetops, keeping ahead of the jeeps, waiting for the next clearing. Chad knew he could not stop or the helicopter would be able to come lower through the sparse trees. Their only hope was to keep moving.

Both Dave and Keeva picked up the rifles they had retrieved from the fallen guards. Dave fumbled a little trying to hold his rifle with the hand of his injured arm. The jostling of the jeep was too much for him to hold the rifle steady. He dropped the rifle and pulled out his pistol.

As the jeeps entered another clearing, the helicopter was waiting for them. They could see Johnson training his rifle on them as they approached at a high rate of speed.

Dave and Keeva began firing as they came out of the trees. This took the men in the helicopter by surprise. They weren't expecting the fugitives to have any guns. The pilot quickly pulled the chopper up, which prevented Johnson from returning fire. The third man in the helicopter also had a rifle, but didn't think he was needed — until now.

The chopper then came in behind the jeeps following just above the trees. Staying behind the jeeps made it harder for Dave and Keeva to fire at the helicopter.

Johnson and the other man began firing through the trees, hoping to hit someone. It had become obvious that Johnson's mission was to prevent their escape. However, most of the shots were directed at the second jeep, because Chad had Parker in the jeep with him, tied up and gagged.

The jeeps played 'cat and mouse' with the helicopter for the next two kilometers, moving in and out of clearings and exchanging gunfire.

Chad was worried, because he knew that the tree line was rapidly dwindling. Soon they would be in the lowland marshes where only shrubs and scrub pines would offer any protection. The treacherous terrain would not allow them to go off-road to escape the helicopter. Chad and Elice continued to drive as fast as they could, zigzagging back and forth across the narrow road, trying anything to make it more difficult for Johnson and the other gunmen.

The helicopter swooped in from the west with the sun behind them. The pilot maneuvered the chopper closer than he had been able to do previously. Johnson and the other man opened fire. Bullets whizzed past the fugitives and hit the jeeps. Joslyn, who was sitting next to Jasper, heard a dull thud and saw Jasper jerk slightly. *"No!* Jasper, are you alright?"

"What happened?" Kat yelled from the front passenger seat.

"Jasper's been shot." Joslyn replied. "Jasper, Jasper. Can you hear me?"

Jasper did not reply.

Another flurry of bullets came and the jeep Elice was driving started sputtering. One or more bullets had damaged the engine. They slowed.

Chad saw what had happened through his rear-view mirror and slowed also. They stopped the jeeps in the middle of the road. "Let's scatter," Chad yelled. Chad and Dave yanked Parker out of the jeep and dove for cover.

Everyone jumped out of the jeeps, except Joslyn and Jasper. Joslyn continued to coax the Indian. "Come on, Jasper. Come on." She was crying now.

"Joslyn!" Chad screamed. "Get out of there *now!*"

The helicopter had made the turn and was now swooping in for another round. Johnson and the other gunman started firing. Joslyn was oblivious to the gunfire, crying, and trying to get Jasper awake.

Keeva left his position, dropping his rifle, and darted for the jeep. He ran behind the jeep, reached over, and yanked Joslyn from her seat. They both hit the ground behind the jeep just as the chopper swept over them. Bullets were flying.

As the chopper went over, Chad drew his pistol. He and Dave both fired as many shots as possible in the few seconds they had.

The unknown gunman clutched his chest and fell from the open door, making a loud thud as he hit the ground some distance from the jeep.

As the chopper banked into a right turn and started back towards the fugitives, Chad yelled for everyone to seek cover. Keeva got Joslyn to cover, then pulled his pistol.

They waited as the helicopter made another approach.

Suddenly, the helicopter banked off to the left, away from the fugitives.

Chad was uncertain what was going on. Then, a second helicopter appeared and began chasing the first.

"What the ..." Dave cried out.

The second chopper quickly overtook the first. Both choppers were out of sight. However, the gunfire could be heard above the whining sound of engines and chopper blades.

The sound of a failing engine was heard. Then the loud crash of a helicopter hitting the ground. They looked at each other. The sound of a helicopter got stronger and stronger.

The fugitives anxiously waited to see which chopper was coming for them. Into sight came the second chopper.

The chopper landed near the jeeps, and three men in military fatigues exited the chopper.

Chad motioned the others to stay under cover. Chad stood and approached the men. One of the men acknowledged Chad. "Are you Dr. Gunnings?"

"Yes, are you Major Reed?" Chad asked.

"No. Major Reed was called back. I am Captain Rodriquez from Ft. Richardson. Congressman Masserman sent me to help you and Dr. Morningside. I guess we came at a good time."

"I guess you did. We sure appreciate the assistance. We have some injuries, and perhaps a fatality." Chad motioned to Jasper, slumped over the seat.

Keeva stood nearby as a medic from the helicopter took Jasper's pulse.

The medic looked solemnly at Keeva, then at the Captain, and shook his head.

Chad went to Joslyn who sobbed in his arms.

The Captain went over to Dave and Trapper to check their injuries. After assuring that they were taken care of, he returned to Chad.

Chad looked up from comforting Joslyn. The man you want is over there. His name is Johann Parker. Parker is the one behind all of this grief.

Chad and the Captain walked over to Parker, who had his head hung over his chest with his arms tied behind his back.

"Why? What did you hope to gain from your secret activities?" Chad asked.

Parker looked up and glared at Chad. "What would you know of my world? I was born and raised on this land. It's mine."

"No," Chad replied. "It belongs to the Dena'ina. You and your family have oppressed them enough."

Parker spat and glowered.

"Your insensitivity toward these people extended to their lands. The damage you have done to the streams and surrounding land has seriously altered the entire salmon fishery of the Kenai River Basin. It will take years and careful management to restore the aquatic ecosystem."

"I had a successful mining operation going here," Parker sneered. "Who's gonna close that down when the ore is there for the taking?"

"I think the Dena'ina will – with Congressman Masserman's help. I will show them how the restoration can be done, and the benefits that will be realized as the ecology of the Kenai River recovers."

Chad whirled and walked quickly back to the jeeps.

Keeva helped the medic take Jasper's body to the chopper, then motioned for Trapper and Dave to come with them. The chopper would take them to the hospital for medical attention.

Dave turned to look at Kat. Before he could say anything, she threw herself in his arms and gave him a passionate kiss. She pulled back and gazed into his eyes, from which all tiredness had just disappeared. "You take care, kiddo. I'll see you back in Soldotna."

Dave smiled, gave a slight wave to the others and walked with a buoyant step beside Trapper's tired shuffle to the waiting helicopter.

"This time, I'll make the scrambled eggs," Kat called after him.

Chad put his arm around Elice, smiled at her, then at Kat. "That's quite a man you got there."

"Yes, I guess so. I'd say we both did pretty well, this trip," Kat replied as she looked at Chad and Elice.

"Let's go back to town," Chad said as the four of them climbed into the one remaining jeep. "You girls wanna do any sightseeing along the way?"

"*No!*" Elice, Kat, and Joslyn replied in unison.

Chapter 25

Justice

Chad and Kat walked down the long hallway. The polished marble floor looked like a sheet of ice with multi-colored pebbles embedded just below the surface. As they walked, they could see into the spacious office suites through each of the open doorways, spaced evenly along the corridor. The bustle of activity was reminiscent of any state building where the hurried pace of rule-making and public service always seemed to be behind schedule. When the two reached the office suites that they were looking for, they walked through the open door and were greeted by a young woman who seemed to be waiting for them.

The young woman smiled pleasantly. "The Congressman is waiting for you. Let me show you to his office." The woman then turned and led them through a maze of cubicles and inner offices that made up the Congressman's suite. At the end of the maze was a conspicuous office in the corner that commanded an excellent view of the Knik Arm of Cook Inlet on the west and Ship Creek on the north. This office was used by the Congressman when he was not in the legislative session in Juneau.

The Congressman was looking out the window at Knik Arm, and turned as Chad and Kat entered. The woman softly closed the door behind them. Congressman Masserman smiled and greeted them warmly. "Dr. Jones, it is good to finally meet you. And, Dr. Gunnings, we meet again."

"Yes, Congressman, I am glad to meet with you a second time, and to thank you for coming to our rescue. I am sorry about Two Feathers. He was a great warrior. And, we would likely not be here today if he and Keeva had not shown up when they did."

"Thank you, Dr. Gunnings." Masserman motioned them to sit at a small table in the corner of his office. "Both Keeva and Two Feathers knew the dangers when they volunteered to find you and to offer to help."

"But they said you had sent them."

"Well, yes. However, I would not have sent them at all, if they had not volunteered."

Masserman turned to Kat. "However, we did not know you were also in the area with an expedition, Dr. Jones."

Kat shrugged. "I didn't think it was necessary to publicize I was conducting an expedition. I also didn't realize that Chad was here, too. Our mutual sponsors thought it prudent to keep that information from both of us."

"Yes, I had a telephone conversation with Sir Hilary not long after you escaped from Parker. He said, that at the time you two began your expeditions, there was enough to worry about without worrying about each other. Besides, he thought you two were in different parts of the Kenai Peninsula." Masserman smiled at Kat. "Dr. Jones, if it hadn't been for your meeting Dave Parsons, who took you on a different course from where you had started, you would have probably not stumbled upon Dr. Gunnings' camp."

Kat looked at Chad. "I guess you are right. However, Chad and I are used to these predicaments, and I would have been chagrined to have missed this one."

Chad gave Kat a surprised look, then saw her grinning at him.

Chad turned to Masserman. "Why didn't you tell Elice and I about Parker the last time we met. You were so secretive, that we suspicioned you were behind the mystery."

Masserman looked at his fingernails briefly before answering. "At our last meeting, I did not know that Parker was a likely suspect. I was trying to protect the interests of the Native associations, and Parker was hiding behind the Dena'ina."

Chad gave Masserman a puzzled look.

"You see, lobbyists for the commercial loggers were claiming that the environmental problems with the salmon fishery was due to the native logging practices, which they claimed were not as environmentally friendly as those of the commercial enterprises. The debate got pretty heated. That's when the Warrior Society sent Keeva and Two Feathers to help me. We initially thought you, Dr. Gunnings, had been hired by the commercial companies to come in and gin up some scientific evidence that would be harmful to the Native associations."

"But, didn't Senator Hodges tell you otherwise?"

"No, and I didn't realize he was connected with PERI. I have to admit that I questioned my own doubts about you when I learned you were collaborating with Dr. Morningside. I could not believe that she would betray her own people."

"So," Chad cleared his throat. "When Elice and I met with you..."

Masserman interrupted him. "When we met, I was very cautious of what I would tell you, even with my doubts. It was not until later, after I had researched PERI, that I realized your institute would never endorse a biased study such as I was suspecting."

Chad and Kat exchanged relieved glances.

"That's when I decided that I needed to help you. I figured that you were in more danger than you realized."

Masserman stood and walked to the window. "And, now its time for me to thank you for your help in discovering and confirming who the real culprit was in this whole mess."

Chad was thoughtful for a moment. "Now that you have Parker. What happens now?"

"Parker will have to answer to a lot of charges. First, and foremost, is his human rights violation and the way he mistreated the Dena'ina. He violated their trust, used their young men to do his dirty work, and stole from them. He will be held accountable for the murders of Two Feathers and Jasper. Second, the environmental damage to the Kenai River Basin is substantial, and restoration will not be easy to accomplish. My next duty is to see that proper restoration is implemented. I could certainly use help from both of you to develop a restoration goal for the Kenai."

"I will be revising my earlier environmental report to include all of my new information," Kat said. "In light of what we know now, I will be sure to include my recommendations."

Chad said, "I am sure that Sir Hilary and Senator Hodges will want PERI to have an active role in prescribing the appropriate restoration for the Kenai. The salmon fishery in this area is critical to the overall ecology of the river basin and to the maintaining of viable salmon populations. This cannot happen if their spawning grounds are made unusable by the tremendous sediment loads from the mining. Now that the mining is stopped, the proactive step is to protect the headwater streams from further soil erosion. I will write up my recommendations, as well, and work with Kat to give you the best plan we can muster."

"Thank you." Masserman said. "I am very much relieved that this matter is coming to a satisfactory conclusion, and I am glad we have come to an equally satisfactory understanding of each other."

"Yes," Chad said as he gazed out the window. "Jasper and Two Feathers would be proud, wouldn't they?"

Epilogue

A somber occasion it was. Chad, Elice, Dave, and Kat sat in a small coffee shop in Anchorage. The tables were small, so Chad and Elice sat at one, and Kat and Dave sat at another. This arrangement was convenient, for two private conversations were taking place.

They were waiting for Joslyn and Don who were doing some last-minute souvenir shopping. Trapper had disappeared once again into the wilderness, refusing to come near the civilization known as Anchorage, and leaving the hospital well before the doctors would have liked.

Dave was lazily stirring his coffee. "Would you ever consider coming to Alaska?" he asked.

"Would you ever consider leaving?" Kat asked.

"I guess so. But, what would I do?" Dave asked.

"Well, I think that either of us radically changing our lives is not a good idea," Kat said as she reached for his hand. Dave looked up from his coffee and into her blue eyes. She continued. "Although we have been through a lot together in the last couple of weeks, we really have just met. It's strange. I feel like I have gotten to know you better in the short time we have been together than I have other men I've known all my life."

"There is a large part of me that doesn't want to lose this — this feeling." Dave shifted uncomfortably in his seat. "On the other hand, I might be out of my element if I were to leave here. Then our relationship would change dramatically." There was silence for a time. "I would like to see you again. Perhaps you could arrange to come here again — soon?"

"Perhaps you could come to California, too. I would like to see you again, Dave," Kat said.

Dave smiled at the invitation. "Yes, I believe the California sun could do me some good." Although, he wasn't really thinking about the sun!

"What do you think will happen to Parker?" Elice asked of Chad.

"Dave took control of the situation with the state police," Chad replied. "He talked directly with the Commissioner about Parker and also Johnson."

"Congressman Masserman worked with Dave and the Commissioner to ferret out other officers who were being paid off by Parker. I'm glad the Congressman turned out to be one of the good guys. I would hate to see Alaskan politics be so corrupt."

"As for Parker, he will be brought up on charges for murder, attempted murder, human rights violations, illegal mining, and environmental damages. Parker's mining activities were causing the major sediment loads downstream in the Kenai watershed, which had drastically affected the natural spawning grounds of the salmon. The Congressman was pleased to know that the problem was not due to the Dena'ina or to the commercial logging companies. He had closed down the commercial operations in order to get to the bottom of the problem. The Congressman is initiating a stream restoration program of the area."

"That's good. I'm glad the Dena'ina will not be held responsible." Elice looked out the window and watched a couple of tourists walk across the street to another shop. The tourist season was coming to an end. Very few tourists were left in the city. Elice turned back to Chad.

"What about the police corruption?"

"The Commissioner promised to conduct an internal investigation of his police force. He was pretty upset with the idea that some of his officers were being paid by Parker."

Elice and Chad sat quietly, sipping their coffee — both lost in thought.

"Keeva stopped by briefly to say goodbye," Elice said.

"Oh?" Chad asked.

"He left to go back to Canada, but wanted to tell me that he thought I would be good at working with the Natives here. He wanted to know whether I would consider leaving the university."

"What did you tell him?"

"I'm happy with my career, and that I will always work with my people to improve their way of life. I didn't see the two as a conflict."

"I think you're right, Elice," Chad said. "Your work here at the university is important. And, hopefully, Parker was a rare breed here in Alaska taking advantage of the Natives with his money-making enterprise."

"What happens now?" Elice asked.

"Well, I guess the Dena'ina will be looking for a new logging coordinator."

Elice looked into Chad's eyes. "No, I mean us."

"Oh ... I've been thinking about that, too." Chad reached for Elice's hand. He gently caressed her hand as he thought about his next words. "We have been through a lot together. From one

273

adventure to the next, we get to know each other better and better." Chad paused as he stared into Elice's bright, brown eyes. "I would take you anywhere." Chad paused, then continued. "I'm not anxious to leave now. I don't know when I'll be back."

Elice looked down at her hands. "Perhaps we shouldn't have gotten involved. There's no future for two people who live in different parts of the world."

"Haven't you heard the world's getting smaller?" Chad quipped, hoping to brighten the situation. It didn't work.

"Our world is still too large. I don't like feeling this way — in love with a man I may not see for long periods of time. Perhaps your previous girlfriend was right. This is no way to have a relationship."

This last statement cut Chad deeply. Maybe he shouldn't become involved with someone, because all he could promise was fleeting moments of time together.

"Chad, I am falling in love with you. But, I am in a professional career — as you are. We both know what that means to personal relationships. I don't think we should jeopardize the good parts of our relationship by dwelling on the bad parts. Let's accept what we have and enjoy each other's company. I don't want to lose that part of our relationship."

Chad's smile returned. "You're right, you know. You sound like me talking. I certainly don't want to lose what I have with you. Cheers!" Chad clinked his coffee cup to Elice's as they both smiled and looked into each other's eyes.

Joslyn and Don burst through the door of the cafe, all out of breath. "Sorry we're late. But I had trouble making up my mind over the mastodon ivory earrings or necklace. They were both so beautiful."

"Which did you buy?" Elice asked.

"I bought them both!" Joslyn replied.

"Come on. We're going to be late for our plane."

Dave and Kat had already gotten up from their table and came over to stand by the others.

"I've decided to stay here for a while," Chad said. Everyone gave Chad a surprised look. Then, a small smile appeared on Elice's face.

Joslyn sputtered. "But, what will Sir Hilary say? I think he has another assignment for us." When she saw the way Elice was looking at Chad, she understood. "Of course, I can always tell him you missed the plane — and several after that!"